antique collecting with BP

VOLUME TWO

by Judith Parkes

Published for the BP Retail Market Division of Shell-Mex and B.P. Ltd by Kenneth Mason

First published 1967, second edition 1969. Book designed
by Sadlergraphics, illustrated by Patricia Mahoney
and printed in England by The Southern Publishing Co Ltd.
Published for the BP Retail Market Division of
Shell-Mex and B.P. Ltd by Kenneth Mason
Publications Ltd, 13–14 Homewell, Havant
Hampshire · Havant 6262–3

Acknowledgements

The author offers her grateful thanks to the
following specialist contributors: **George
Savage** author of many books on ceramics, for
his introduction to the ceramic chapter; **Peter
Philp** for his introduction to the furniture chapter;
and **Tony Keniston** for his contribution to the reviews
of furniture dealers throughout; **Robinsons Bookshop,
Brighton** for their help with the book lists; **The Antique
Finder** for advice and help in compiling the glossary of
dealers. The cover photograph was taken at the stands
of Moreton Antiques Ltd (furniture), Oliver Sutton
(ceramics) and Sladmore Gallery (bronzes), all at
the Antique Hypermarket, London W8

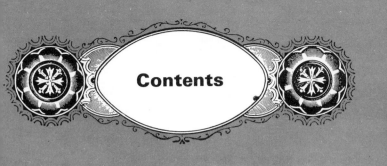

Contents

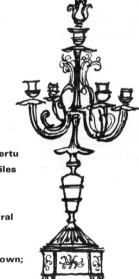

Antiques

— how the trade works in Britain

During the past fifteen years the antiques trade has expanded by about 5 per cent every year so that whereas in 1950 there were about 1000 established dealers, the figure is now more than 3000. This expansion is due to several factors, the main ones being the increasing popularity of antiques and collecting in general and the steady rise in prices keeping pace with inflation. The British antique trade has been particularly buoyant over the past two or three years due to enormous foreign interest in our wares. Compared with America and Europe, prices in Great Britain suggest our antiques are undervalued. The British public often resents having to pay what is considered a high price for a piece of antique furniture, but is blissfully ignorant of what that piece might fetch in Italy or France. Small wonder that so much of our heritage is finding its way abroad, and who can blame the dealers for letting it go? By the time we have woken up to the fact that it is often cheaper to buy a Regency dining chair than it is to buy a brand new one, there will be precious few left to buy. The second reason, of course, for the great surge of antiques going overseas, has been devaluation. There were reports of dealers being cleared right out of their stocks, especially silver plate, immediately prior to and just after devaluation. Prices have now found a new but much higher level, and have settled down a bit.

Antique dealers come from all walks of life and as personalities are often fascinating. They range from enthusiastic youngsters with a market stall, sharp young men out to make a quick pound without too many scruples, to retired service families who convert country mansions into elegant antique showrooms. Some dealers buy all their stock from auction rooms, some deal only with a private clientéle, buying locally from a range of contacts built up over the years, some get their stock mainly from other dealers, and some use the services of a 'runner'—a free-lance trader with no overheads who tours the country with an estate car or sometimes just a zip bag, buying a wide range of fairly low-priced antiques for resale the same week either at one of the London markets or to dealers with whom he has arranged to supply certain well defined items.

All dealers, whether comparative newcomers or old hands share one thing: deep personal regard and feeling for the beautiful, the rare and the unusual. It is this personal interest in his wares which makes the antique dealer more of an individualist than the average retail shopkeeper. To start with, he cannot pick up a telephone and order a dozen or so of this and that. He has to go out and search for his stock, relying on his flair and knowledge to buy at a price which will show him a reasonable profit margin. He has to eat like everyone else, and finding stock at the right price is the biggest problem he faces, for the retailer has to compete directly with the public when buying. He has only three sources of supply – the general public, the auction room, and his fellow traders. It is not unusual, therefore, for a piece to change hands several times within the trade before it is sold to a private collector. A piece might be bought privately and inexpensively by Smith who realised its potential but who had no local demand for such an item. Smith would be happy to sell at a small profit to Jones who fancied it but was glad to take a small margin when it was bought by Brown a week later who had been searching in vain for such a piece. Brown would again be happy with a small profit to maintain his goodwill with a long-standing customer who had asked him to keep his eyes open for such an item of which he was building a collection.

Another misconception of the antique trade concerns the large profit margins that some dealers occasionally make. This can occur for example, if a knowledgeable dealer makes an un-opposed bid for a good piece at an out-of-the-way country auction on a foggy day. The locals may not realise its value but the visting dealer does because of his hard-earned knowledge. Now it is quite obvious that in such a case a dealer who has paid only £5 for a piece worth more than £50 will sell at the latter

price because it is the replacement value which the trade must consider when selling an item, not the actual cost. This is also the reason why you may be astonished to find that a dealer stubbornly refuses to bargain with you over an unusual piece and flatly will not reduce his price. It isn't that he doesn't want to sell the item, he most certainly does, but he knows he cannot replace it at the price you are offering him and he is also safe in the knowledge that it is worth what he is asking and that before long he will get it.

On another day the same dealer may travel 200 miles to a country sale and come back empty handed or be called to a distant private home to view some Sheraton furniture which turns out to be Edwardian. So, naturally, an antique dealer must play swings and roundabouts with his individual profit margins to average a net return comparable to his fellow retailer's, after covering his travelling expenses which can be considerable.

The major question that haunts the unknowledgeable seeker of antiques is undoubtedly 'is it genuine?' The importance of gaining the confidence of the collector was recognised in 1918 when the British Antique Dealers Association was formed to raise the status of the trade by fostering goodwill between their members and the public. Members of this association would not risk their reputation lightly by making false or irresponsible attributions and the association will always arrange for independent arbitration in case of doubt. Even apart from the 500 or so members of BADA the great majority of genuine antique dealers are also intent on building up their goodwill and it is contrary to their interests to make false claims. Naturally, as in every trade, there are exceptions and the beginner must remember the legal maxim – *caveat emptor*, ('let the buyer beware'). In law, the buyer is entitled to rely on the dealer to sell him something of the nature and quality of the thing demanded and if the asking price is paid on the strength of the dealer's representation (not the buyer's judgement) then the goods can be returned and a refund demanded. In practice most reputable dealers will be only too happy to give a full description of the article on the invoice with a statement to the effect that he undertakes to repurchase the article for the same price if it is proved to be inaccurately described.

One last legal aspect of the antique trade is the bogey of auction rings. A ring is formed by a group of dealers who attend an auction sale having previously agreed not to bid against each other for certain lots, and then hold a second auction between themselves. The difference between the price paid at the first auction and that at the second 'private' auction is shared between the participating dealers. This practice is known as a 'knockout' or 'settlement'. This is, of course, illegal insomuch as those who take part are said to have formed a conspiracy to defraud the vendor.

This practice is legalised, however, if the traders concerned notify the auctioneer prior to the sale, that they are buying as a syndicate. This is seldom done. Ring dealers claim that if the seller is too mean or too stupid to pay for a proper valuation of his goods, resulting in an inadequate reserve price, there is no reason why the dealer should share his hard-earned professional knowledge by bidding against his fellow traders in order to enrich the seller.

The dealers present at an auction sale are often the only people who know the true value of certain pieces and they consider that this knowledge should be rewarded. 'After all', they argue, 'you have to pay for the services of a doctor or lawyer, so if you will not pay us to value your goods, why expect us to give you the full value at the expense of our colleagues?'

Many dealers who once took part in these settlements on the grounds that all is fair under the hammer, were among the most scrupulous in their direct dealing with the public, often paying a private seller a better price than they would pay at an auction and maintaining the highest standard of integrity regarding the correct attribution and authenticity of their wares. Their motto has always been 'My first duty is to my customer. If he trusts me he will have a fair deal. If he sends goods to the salerooms to make me compete with the public and my fellow dealers, then I shall bid as low as possible.'

National press publicity, followed by BADA's new rule as a condition of membership forbidding its members to participate in any form of settlement, combined with talk of Government action, has resulted in the diminution if not complete cessation of organised rings and it is to be hoped that this state of affairs will continue.

Be a good customer . . .

While visiting dealers for inclusion in this second edition of the guide, I have been struck by a change in the trade's attitude when dealing with the public. A few years ago the majority of dealers were rather cheery people, pleasant, courteous and trusting. Nowadays it is sometimes the case that the customer who enters a shop for the first time not only meets with a disinterest bordering on hostility, but when he comes to buy something is made to feel almost unwelcome.

During the last few years the antique trade has taken some hard knocks. First there was the publicity given to the rings which brought disrepute to the innocent as well as to the guilty.

Then came the 'phoney dealer' scandal. Pairs of supposed traders who turned up with lorries, bought large quantities of valuable stock and paid with dud cheques, often causing ruin to the dealer concerned. Last, the increasing difficulty in finding replacement stock, which is serious for the trade as a whole and is forcing some smaller dealers out of business. It is heartbreaking for a long-established dealer of high reputation to find

himself forced to stock a quantity of Victorian items or heavily restored pieces. Such dealers rightly believe the whole nature of their business is changing.

Inevitably the discontent which is aroused by this situation rubs off onto the customer. When you walk into an antique shop today and are unknown to the dealer concerned, you could be one of four types of people. First you could be, and he hopes you will be, a bona fide customer looking genuinely for a particular piece of furniture or collector's item. Secondly, you could be another dealer, in which case there's a good chance he's going to make some kind of a sale.

Thirdly, you could be a browser who is going to walk round for half an hour, pick up everything in the shop, ask a lot of unintelligent questions and then buy nothing. A few years ago this was OK and all part of the game. The dealer didn't mind because he was by nature a friendly person, and so interested in his business that it was a joy to him to share his knowledge with you. This is still the case with a large proportion of the trade thank goodness – but the treasure hunter will occasionally be faced with the other kind and it's as well to understand his point of view. Nowadays it can be a major irritant to an important dealer to have to waste time on browsers. Some businesses have recently closed their doors to the general public and are open only to the trade with whom they found themselves already doing 80 per cent of their business whilst they had their doors open to the private customer as well. Now they find that their stock can't be replaced and is likely to be sold to an overseas buyer or other dealer anyway they do not want to waste time unnecessarily.

Fourthly, you could be a confidence man. The antique trade has received far more than its fair share of confidence tricksters in the last few years. And it is difficult for them when an unknown customer wishes to make a relatively expensive purchase. Quite often a bona fide private buyer is far from home when he sees the piece he wants and it is inconvenient for him not to take the goods with him, especially if it is either large furniture, or fragile glass. Then the dealer has to decide whether he dares accept a cheque and lose sight of the goods before it is cleared. If he

Bygones displayed like this at Dunnings Antiques of St Albans, are decorative as well as valuable

insists on cash he may lose the sale, because few people carry large quantities of money around with them. The trade themselves usually take cash when they go on a buying tour – they understand the dilemma. But the average customer doesn't always get the point and is often quite upset at any hesitation on the dealer's part to accept a cheque.

So when you go out looking for antiques – do try and see the dealer's point of view should you encounter any reluctance on his part to be obliging. If you want to browse, say so. He probably won't mind at all – he'll certainly mind far less than if you try to fool him for half an hour that you *just might* be interested in almost everything in the shop.

Don't be depressed by this attitude, just plough on regardless. Most dealers are aware that today's thirty bob teaspoon buyer may be tomorrow's hundred guinea baluster goblet collector, or even the author of a collector's guide!

If you seriously think you might buy something on a day's treasure-hunting, take cash with you, or offer to leave the goods until a cheque is cleared. The fact that you thought to offer may well be enough to underwrite your honesty!

Enjoy your antiques now – and pay later!

I am sure there are many occasions when you have longed to own a particular piece of furniture, but it's been just too expensive to write out a cheque there and then. The sight of the most divine *bonheur du jour*, almost inevitably will clash with a bill for the school fees, and guess what has to give way? It seems fantastic that it's taken so long for someone to realise the potential in the need for credit to cover the cost of antiques, but at last all the

snags and pitfalls which used to make finance companies wary of such an enterprise have been ironed out, and it is now possible to buy antiques on the never-never.

One scheme on the market, is not strictly hire-purchase but extended credit terms. It is easy for both customer and dealer to use the scheme, which in simple language works like this:

You go into the shop, spot the goods and agree with the dealer that he is willing for you to purchase them on extended credit terms.

You and the dealer together fill in a proposal form which describes the goods, gives details of vendor and buyer (*ie* name address, banker's reference etc), and full purchase price of the article.

The proposal form is sent to head office where the references and authenticity of the goods are checked and the credit agreement prepared.

The form of agreement is sent to the dealer. You go in and sign it, pay your deposit and take away your purchase.

The whole exercise will take about seven days depending how prompt you are in completing and signing the forms. Details of this scheme and proposal forms from The Antique Finance Plan Ltd, 72 Rochester Row, London SW1, Telephone 01-828 5977/8

Don't expect to strike a hard price bargain, and *then* ask for credit terms – you should check first – that the dealer is willing to co-operate. Any good service has to be paid for, so the trader cannot be expected to give a rock bottom price, as well as provide credit facilities.

Interest rates are approximately the same as for buying a car and the maximum repayment period is 24 months. Initial deposit is 25 per cent. Although these details are correct at the time of going to print, they are subject to government legislation. You should check the up-to-date situation before signing your agreement.

Chapter one

furniture – fourteenth to nineteenth century

Basically, there are two ways to set about buying antique furniture. The first is to stay put at a favourite spot, and wait for the goodies to arrive. The favourite spot, for many, is one or other of the leading salerooms, and some people seem to do quite well be haunting them. There is little truth, however, in the legend that these auctioneers offer demi-pension terms to their regular customers! The great advantage, and also the chief snag, with this static method of buying is that everything is expertly appraised before it is offered for sale. The catalogue descriptions are as accurate as possible, which is fine for those unable to classify the goods for themselves. Against this is the fact that most of the competition comes from professionals who know values down to the last shilling, and it is only rarely that a bargain is likely to fall into an amateur lap.

The other way is to search far and wide. This uses up more petrol, demands more knowledge, tends to be more of a gamble but – if you enjoy travelling anyway – is much more fun.

The French have two words for furniture *meubles* and *mobiliers* and both have the same secondary meaning: mobile. And that, more than anything else, is what the keen buyer of antique furniture has to be. Unless he is mobile to a high degree, the fine pieces will move around faster than he does, and always elude him.

Knowledge can be acquired in a number of ways. One is to attend first-class, well-catalogued auction sales as an observer, noting the subtle differences in superficially similar pieces – differences that command high bids. Auction rooms allow the **17** browser a remarkably free reign in examining even valuable lots. Watch the experts at work. To see an authority on French furniture, for instance, examine the construction of a commode is an education.

Furniture can be understood thoroughly only if examined with the greatest care. Apart from reproduction and clever fakes – some old enough to have acquired a deceptive patina – there is a vast number of made-up pieces in circulation. These are partly genuine, partly not. Many over-large, unsaleable articles have been cut down to size. New stands have been supplied to such things as tallboy chests.

Three Chippendale chairs may have been knocked apart, to reappear magically as a set of six – each one being half genuine, half 'restored'. Such things may still be worthy furnishing items, but if they are being offered as completely period, with price-tag to match, then watch it. The reputable dealer will always point out such modifications, and the intelligent collector will always take a particular interest in them instead of hurrying past the moment he is told the piece is not pure. This sort of piece provides a wonderful object lesson, and there is as much to be learned from the piece that is wrong as from that which is right.

There is also a great deal to be learned from the dealer – but he must be a right one, too. The dealer who is at, or near, the top of

his particular tree is entitled to charge a price based not only on the article itself, but to some extent, on his own expertise. He is selling, not just chattels, but scholarship, and included in the price is his professional fee. The would-be collector who is really ignorant is well advised to pay this slightly higher price, and obtain the advice and the guarantee that the reliable dealer can offer. Most good traders are ready to share their knowledge with their customers, even though they may be making future competitors for themselves in the open market.

Museums offer another means of acquiring knowledge, though not of examining things in detail, unless special permission is obtained. Curators will usually offer facilities for handling exhibits in their presence, and chat about them with erudition if the enthusiast takes the trouble to write in advance, asking for such an opportunity.

Book learning is not to be despised, either, though the lessons to be learned are mainly those which lead to a thorough understanding of style, which alone is insufficient to judge authenticity. What the intelligent reader learns is to recognise the period to which a piece purports to belong. He must supplement this with practical guidance from someone really expert, who will not only sort out the clever copy, but also put into their true perspective any features in a genuine piece which appear, misleadingly, to be out of period stylistically.

Anachronisms do not always mean that a piece is not genuine. Country-made pieces often suffer from hangovers from an earlier period, because the village craftsman was not fully abreast of metropolitan fashion and tried to blend what he understood of it with what he had learned, perhaps half-a-century before, when serving his apprenticeship.

In Yorkshire, for example, you will often see oak chairs with backs in the Chippendale style, but with turned legs and underframing reminiscent of the previous century. These are country bumpkins that have to be dated according to the latest designfeature discernible. At their own level – and often it is no mean one – they can be desirable items. Cottage furniture does not appear all that often in the more important London salerooms, and it is best studied with the help of country dealers who have specialized in it and learned about local traditions and idio-syncrasies.

Only the observant traveller learns to detect and relish local flavours, often too subtle to describe or even to draw. One may learn from a book – or from a dealer – how the Dutch joined the underframing of chairs; how the Danes left the upper edge of the drawer-front and the Parisians that of a drawer-side; the correct shape for the keyholes on a Georgian chest of drawers and the proper position of the dowel-pins in a Commonwealth joint-stool; but many differences are so much less definite, so much a matter of national or local feeling.

A potted history of furniture

Gothic 1300–1550
Really nothing to do with the Goths. Mediaeval style, current throughout Europe over a long period. Chiefly oak, but any available timber used, depending on locality. Not much domestic furniture in use, most that survives shows influence of Gothic church architecture, especially in carved decoration. Character-istic pieces: chests of plank construction, massive 'refectory' tables on trestles, hutches, solid-ended stools.

Renaissance and Baroque 1400–1740
Overlaps Gothic. The Renaissance began in Italy, spread slowly northwards. A decorated style owing something to renewed interest in Greek and Roman culture and taking on national characteristics. Developed into heavy, ornate Baroque, carried to extreme in France under Louis xiv and persisting longer in Germany than elsewhere. Rich carving, elaborate turning, heavy geometrical mouldings. Italians inlaid with marble and other stones, Portuguese with pewter patterns. French inlaid brass arabesques into tortoiseshell veneer banded with ebony

Mrs Bellis has her Hungerford house furnished in Gothic, 16th and 17th century style. Some family living rooms are her showrooms!

(Buhlwork). English developed from robust Elizabethan, through severe Commonwealth to imported French and Dutch designs following restoration of the monarchy, when marquetry decoration on walnut ground became fashionable. Characteristic pieces: cabinets or drawers on stands, richly carved armchairs with velvet upholstery.

Rococo 1730–1760
Invented by an Italian but essentially French, reaching its zenith under Louis xv. A development from, and also a reaction against, the Baroques. Delicate, feminine, employing snaky, curving lines (serpentine) wherever possible. At its best, incomparably elegant; at its worst, absurdly asymmetrical. English Rococo developed by Chippendale and his followers, mostly in rather restrained fashion, but occasionally out-rocking the continental Rococo, *eg* Chinese Chippendale. Characteristic pieces: anything with cabriole legs (s-curves). Favourite woods: kingwood in France, mahogany in England.

Neo-classic (first phase) 1760–1820
Fed up with Rococo curves, designers found inspiration in the revival of interest (previously felt during the Renaissance) in classical architecture. Return to discipline brought about **21**

Louis XVI style in France and Adam style in Britain, both of which influenced rest of Europe.

Snaky line was out, only permitted curves being circles and elipses, with great emphasis on slim, vertical line characterised by use of classical column. Favourite motifs: ram's heads, acanthus leaves, trophies of arms. Lightness in construction and colour, with satinwood – inlaid or painted – used for high-grade furniture. Chippendale adapted this manner and worked under Adam. Hepplewhite adopted and modified the style to suit domestic requirements, Sheraton picked up the rear end of eighteenth century. All these names are convenient labels used to indicate style and period, and seldom imply identity of actual maker. Characteristic pieces: semi-eliptical commodes (side-boards, if you like – not night-commodes!); lyre and shield-back chairs, Pembroke tables with delicately tapered, vertical legs.

Neo-classic (second phase)

Known as Empire on continent and as English Empire (not British Empire) or Regency in Britain. In France, largely a style to glorify Napoleon's empire. In England, an equally solemn effort to evolve a classical style different from, and more solid than, Adam's. Employed Egyptian, Greek and Roman ideas. Emphasis on horizontal line and use of concave curve for legs (now known as sabre or Trafalgar legs). Chief designers: Percier and Fontaine in France and Holland, and Hope in England. Favourite woods; mahogany and rosewood. Characteristic pieces: Mme Recamier sofas, low bookcases with metal-grille doors.

Romantic 1820–1910

Empire style degenerated in Austrian Biedermeier – substantial, middle-class and ingenious in its use of swan's legs as arms for sofas (carved, not real, swans). Soon got mixed up with all the romantic revivals of earlier styles that occurred throughout nineteenth century and after. The Victorians produced their own versions of Gothic, Baroque, Rococo and Classical, often mixing them all together and adding a few more ingredients of their own devising. Towards end of century came two related revolts against decline into vulgarity; the William Morris school of craftsmen making cottage designs by hand, in solid oak with enormous copper hinges; and art nouveau – originally a British fantasy which got dressed up into something even more fanciful by Viennese and Parisian designers. Favourite woods: the lot. Characteristic pieces: brass bedsteads, horsehair sofas, papier maché tables, incredible sideboards, well-shaped button-back chairs.

A quick ready-reckoner to dates, periods and furniture styles

Dates of accession of Kings and Queens of England

1509 Henry VIII
1547 Edward VI
1553 Mary
1558 Elizabeth
1603 James I
1649 Commonwealth (Cromwell)
1660 Charles II
1685 James II
1689 William and Mary
1702 Anne
1714 George I
1727 George II
1760 George III
1820 George IV
1830 William IV
1837 Victoria
1901 Edward VII

Dates of periods and important furniture styles

1330-1550 Gothic
1485-1588 Tudor

1558-1603 Elizabethan
1603-1649 Jacobean
1649-1660 Cromwellian
1660-1688 Carolean
1689-1702 William and Mary
1702-1714 Queen Anne
1714-1800 Georgian
1749-1779 Chippendale
1762-1792 Adam
1775-1800 Heppelwhite
1785-1805 Sheraton
1800-1820 Regency
1837-1901 Victorian
1901-19 Edwardian

23

Books to read

Adam and Hepplewhite and other neo-classical furniture C Musgrave Faber 63s

Antique English furniture The Connoisseur New Guide 35s

Antique furniture J McDonald Collins 6s

Antique furniture for the smaller home P Philp Arco 15s

Antiques in their periods H Gordon Murray 7s 6d and 15s

The art of furniture Wanscher Allen and Unwin 120s

British furniture throughout the ages K Middlemas Weidenfeld 25s

Cabinet and chairmaker's real friend 1965 R Manwaring Tiranti 6s

Chippendale furniture A Goleridge Faber 110s

Chippendale furniture designs R Symonds Tiranti 10s 6d

Complete guide to furniture styles Boger Allen and Unwin 105s

Connoisseur's complete period guide R Edwards Connoisseur 84s

A short dictionary of furniture J Gloag Allen and Unwin 105s

Empire furniture S Grandjean Faber 84s

The encyclopaedia of furniture J Aronson Batsford 63s

A history of English furniture E Joy Country Life 18s

English furniture J Gloag Black 30s

English furniture E T Joy Batsford 21s

English furniture J Rogers Spring 25s

English furniture J Rogers Country Life 45s

English furniture of the Georgian period M Jourdain Country Life 63s

English furniture of the 18th century D Nickerson Weidenfeld 30s

English furniture styles 1500-1830 R Fastnedge Penguin 10s 6d

The Englishman's chair J Gloag Allen and Unwin 63s

French royal furniture P Verlet Barrie 90s

French 18th century furniture H Landais Weidenfeld 30s

French 19th century furniture G Souchel Weidenfeld 37s 6d

Furniture: an explanatory history D Reeves Faber 12s 6d

Furniture collecting for amateurs J Henderson Muller 18s

Where to buy

Furniture

There are nearly a thousand general furniture dealers in London and to mention them all individually would require a separate guide. For a comprehensive list of these dealers with their stock fully described see *The British Antiques Yearbook*. The trade in London tends to be concentrated into half a dozen different areas; in some cases there are twenty to thirty dealers in one street.

Camden Passage (N1)

About thirty dealers with permanent shops concentrated in a new arcade and adjoining premises. Some 20–30 stalls on Saturdays (see chapter six, Antique markets volume one). Parking, side streets to the east. Early closing, normally Thursday.

Camden High Street and Chalk Farm Road (NW1)

About twenty dealers with permanent shops within a quarter of a mile. Good selections of furniture. Parking: usually room in the side streets. Early closing, normally Thursday.

Baker Street (W1)

About 100 dealers in small shops in most of the streets off Baker St, such as George St and Blandford St (many of them are specialists and mentioned in other sections). This area includes many large emporiums such as *Antique City* with a large selection of stripped pine furniture. Early closing in this area, normally Saturday.

Kensington Church Street (W8)

At least forty dealers with good quality general stock in a quarter of a mile walk. Parking, side streets on the west side, but becoming more difficult. The *Antique Hypermarket* is here (see volume one). Early closing, normally Thursday.

Portobello Road and Westbourne Grove (W11)

More than 100 dealers with permanent shops augmented to 500 or more on Saturdays when the famous market operates. (see volume one). Mostly inexpensive furniture, oak, pine and Victorian pieces. The home of what is now described as trad, but really bygones of the Victorian and Edwardian periods. Parking, reasonably easy, in side streets all around. Early closing, normally Thursday.

Bond Street and the West End (W1 SW1)

Leading antique dealers of international repute located within a square mile. Also the big sale rooms of Sotheby's and Christie's. Meter parking at 2s per hour or for a longer session the underground car park in Hyde Park or multi-storey garage in Old Burlington St. Early closing, normally Saturday.

Knightsbridge, Chelsea, Fulham Road (SW3, SW5, SW6, SW7, SW10)

Starting from Harrods in Knightsbridge, SW3, there are several hundred dealers in a three mile corridor running in a south-westerly direction, on or near three main streets running parallel to each other – Brompton Rd, Fulham Rd and King's Rd. Also

Sloane St running north-south down to *Peter Jones* antique furniture department in Sloane Square at the top of King's Rd. Prices (and, up to a point, the quality of the goods) tend to get lower as one approaches the Fulham end and the Earl's Court Rd. Do the tour in three stages. Early closing Saturday in Knightsbridge, Sloane St and easterly end of Brompton Rd, otherwise normally Thursday.

Some specialist dealers in London

Eighteenth century English and Regency furniture

WC1 M Harris
NW1 W R Harvey
W1 H W Keil, Mann & Fleming, H Blairman, Mallett, Frank Partridge, Temple Williams Ltd, Ayer, Aspreys of Bond St, Fortnum & Mason
W8 Church St Galleries
SW1 Clifford Dade, Glaisher & Nash, Geoffrey Rose Ltd, Spink Denys Wrey, Peter Jones (4th floor) Harrods
SW3 Norman Adams, John Keil, Peter Bernard, David Tron, A F Fredericks, Gloria Antica, Jeremy, David Tremayne

SW5 Gerald Spyer
SW7 C Fredericks
NW3 Dolphin Antiques
SW10 Brooks Gillingham, Hamish (London) Ltd

Continental furniture

WC1 M Harris
W1 A Cook, Fisher Gallery, Mallett at Bourdon House, Frank Partridge
W8 Vita Juel
SW3 Villafranca, Jacob Stodel, M Turpin, Chester Antiques

27

SW10 Hamish	**SW6** Avice Mostyn Antiques,
SW1 Au Vieux Paris	Clewes & Makin

Sixteenth and seventeenth century oak furniture	**Pine furniture**
W8 Ivar Mackay	**N1** T & S Lemkow
W11 Giblin & Hirst	**W8** The Lacquer Chest
SW1 Michael Dumez-Onof,	**SW6** Guinevere, Avice Mostyn
Giannitini	**SW7** The Pine Chest
SW3 Ciancimino, R Symes	**W2** R Plitzka Antiques Ltd
	W11 Big Deal, Things

The home counties

One of the finest shops I have visited within an easy drive of London is owned by *John Bly*. Here, all the courtesy and experience of the long-established trader is at the disposal of the private buyer, and above all Mr Bly's prices are reasonable. The more choice pieces are in the main showroom at 50 High St, Berkhamstead, but customers should also ask to be shown to the large barn-showroom at the rear of the shop premises. Approached through a most attractive courtyard filled with flowers (in season) the 'second' showroom has less important pieces including some fine reproduction items such as dining tables made from old wood. Everything in Mr Bly's shop is clearly marked and underwritten by the experience and customer-orientation of the owner who even provides notepads for those customers who wish to jot down measurements, and furniture period dates for the truly innocent. Everything that *can* be done, *is* done, to facilitate the ease and pleasant atmosphere in which an antique purchase should be made.

A must visit for the lover of beautiful Georgian furniture is the shop which *Mrs Norwood* owns at 146 High St, Berkhamstead. Despite the increasing shortage of quality pieces which is the overwhelming problem faced by the long-established dealer, Mrs Norwood will not compromise on quality and would rather have a few fine pieces than a shopful of less distinguished items. At my last visit I saw a beautiful wine cooler, Georgian cheval mirror, and one of the finest D-end dining tables seen for many months. *Park Street Antiques*, 350 High St also has a good range of furniture including at our last visit some lovely decorator's items such as giltwood mirrors and marble-topped console table.

Furniture of all periods is to be found at *Wilkinsons Cottage Antiques*, Hungerford, Berks. These premises live up to their name. A whitewashed cottage is an ideal setting for furniture.

Although *Mrs Margaret Jarvis* has been dealing in antiques since 1917 her enthusiasm for them has not waned. At the High House, Newbury, standing on the right on a corner as the town centre is approached from the west you will see fine quality furniture of the eighteenth century as well as a selection of general antiques.

Right in the middle of Abingdon, Berks is the large premises of *R R Morris*. Always a wide selection of furniture of all periods with other unusual items. Mr Morris has another, but much smaller shop at Sutton Courtenay, a beautiful little country village just a few miles from Abingdon. It's quite easy to drive past the shop by mistake it seems so small, but through the gates is a much larger showroom than can be seen from the road.

Up the fascinating High St at Burford, Oxon, where no house is less than 200 years old, a clock can be seen projecting from the ancient Tolsey which now houses the Town Museum. There are several interesting shops here, especially *Peter Matthey Ltd* whose shop is called The Crypt and is built on the side of an old monastery. As you go into the downstairs showrooms you get that marvellous smell of old stonework, a fitting environ of the good stock of old oak and porcelain offered. Mr Matthey offers customers a card with a crib sheet of dates and furniture styles by period. More oak can be found in the upstairs showroom of *Zene Walker Ltd*, The Bull House, High St, also at the premises of *R Bowerman*, The Antiquary, High St.

Drive into Faringdon, Berks from Abingdon or Oxford, The Faringdon Galleries are on the right, opposite the junction with the road to Wantage. Here *Mr and Mrs Charles Thornton* have built up a fine business which maintains a stock of fine quality eighteenth century and Regency furniture at reasonable prices. Mr Thornton, who speaks five languages and does most of the buying, has exquisite taste which is reflected in all his stock. 'He never has his head out of some antique book or other . . .', complains Mrs Thornton, but her loss is the customer's gain, for not only is he a knowledgeable dealer as a result but is willing to give advice and short instruction to his clients.

Dunstable has many historic associations. Here Watling St crosses the Icknield Way and an eleventh century priory is still in evidence. During the fourteenth and fifteenth centuries the court came from London to watch the jousting and it was the only place Henry viii found it possible to obtain a divorce from

Catherine of Aragon. Alexander Podd was known throughout the antique trade in the 1930's as The Regency King. Thirty years ago when auctioneers catalogued Regency furniture as 'early Victorian', and conventional antique dealers would not look at it, *Mr Podd* filled his Mayfair showrooms with this furniture. Since then he has moved to Dunstable and been joined in business by his son, Henry. *Podd & Son* still try to have a few pieces of Regency furniture in stock. 'But it is always true Regency,' says Henry Podd, 'not George IV or William IV, either with mounts added or heavy carvings subtracted which seems to be the current version of Regency'. Specialists in period interior decoration, Alexander Podd & Son's Dunstable showrooms are ideally suited to the display of a stock which combines the antique, the elegant and the decorative with a predilection for the rare and the unusual. The elegant is exemplified by articles of Hepplewhite and French design; the decorative by japanned furniture, particularly arm chairs and satinwood pieces; and the rare by urns, vases and tazza in Blue John, of which they probably hold the largest stock in the world. Across the broad High St, *W A Pinn* has numerous showrooms stocked with fine eighteenth century furniture and earlier pieces. Pembroke tables, clocks, old oak sets of chairs and inlaid pieces are always among Mr Pinn's varied stock.

In Farnham, Surrey *P & B Jordan* offer an interesting selection of antiques including decorative furniture. A mixed stock so that there is something of interest for every caller.

St Alban's is a real Mecca for the furniture collector. Starting with *Antelope Antiques* in George St, who have fine quality small furniture pieces, going next door to *Josephine Grahame-Ballin* who stocks large pieces in her fifteenth century shop which used to be an inn, then over the road to *James* for more smaller furniture items. Keeping the Cathedral on your right, go up to the traffic lights and turn right for Holywell Hill where there are no less than seven dealers to visit. Near the top *Hepplewhite House*, and *R E Norwood Ltd* both offer fine eighteenth century furniture, *Pillers* at number 15 specialise in early oak and decorative country pieces and *Crispins* at number 37 have an even larger stock of same. Two or three hundred yards down on the left, set back from the road is *Charles Perry* with an outstanding stock of old English furniture.

Bowood Antiques at Wendover Dean, Bucks, tucked away two

hundred yards from the main road between Great Missenden and Wendover, may not be one of the easiest antique shops to find, but a visit can be rewarding. There is always a plentiful supply of Victoriana and earlier furniture plus a variety of general antiques. The stock is housed in two barns and customers are invited to browse at their leisure.

At Taylor House you will find *Chevertons* of Edenbridge. In six showrooms they offer one of the largest stocks of English and continental furniture in the area. The house is attractive, with beams and whitewash and winding staircase to the upstairs showrooms.

It isn't every day that an antique dealer is offered first refusal on the entire contents of a castle. Many dealers dream of such an opportunity, but the dream became reality for *Mrs Mary Bellis* and was the start of the finest stock of Gothic and Renaissance oak furniture to be seen outside a museum. Charnham Close, Hungerford, Berks is a home as well as a shop, where the family live contentedly in a sixteenth century atmosphere. Mrs Bellis can offer you anything from an Elizabethan joint stool to a piece of seventeenth century French church statuary. Panelling, tapestries, court cupboards and four poster beds are merely a few of the items always in stock.

Songs are not for sale, but may well accompany a sale, if you go antique hunting in Watlington, Oxon. Singer *Philadelphia Lee* has given up arias for oak at her shop, The Old Bank House. Welsh farm furniture is always stocked, also some good pictures and small items. Prices are reasonable. Almost next door is *Thimbles Antiques* who stock good small pieces of eighteenth century furniture, and porcelain.

A browserie not to be missed is *Griffons Court*, Highclere near Newbury, Berkshire. Five showrooms of furniture, supplemented by a paradise of a warehouse packed with goodies.

Small items of furniture of beautiful quality make a visit to *Mr and Mrs Littleton* of Crescent Rd, Tunbridge Wells well worth the trip. I saw an exquisite marquetry bombe commode at my last visit in such perfect condition and so fairly priced it was gone in two days! The Littletons are now increasing their stock and have taken over a second showroom just a few doors away, so be sure to visit both premises in case you miss something good!

Tunbridge Wells is such a hotbed of fine antique shops, it is impossible to single out just one dealer. The area in and around **31**

The Pantiles is rich in fine things, and I must recommend *Leonard Strawson* who has the most comprehensive stock of eighteenth and nineteenth century furniture, *Ann Spear* who has a good selection of furniture and a choice of decorative items which do credit to her excellent taste. Also *John Thornton* at The Chair Shop offers comfortable looking antiques at a reasonable price, easy to live with and pleasing to the eye. Just around the corner in Chapel Place is Chapel Antiques Ltd with a magnificent stock of early oak and Renaissance furniture with some early treen.

Merlin Pennink, wife of the designer of golf courses all over the world, is locally renowned for her taste and expertise in interior decor, she can be found at 27 The Pantiles.

Some other dealers in the home counties

Thame, Oxon George Newitt *oak, eighteenth century*
St Albans, Herts Crispins *oak, cottage furniture*
Brasted, Kent P Frank *oak*
Hertford, Herts Beckwith *oak*
Abingdon, Berks R R Morris *eighteenth century*
Canterbury, Kent Old Palace Galleries
Maidenhead, Berks Biggs *eighteenth century*
Guildford, Surrey G Oliver *oak, eighteenth century* ·

Hitchin, Herts Phillips *eighteenth century*
Eton, Bucks Toller *oak* J A Pearson *regency*
Walton-on-the-Hill, Surrey Regency House *eighteenth century, Regency*
Windsor, Berks Nicholas Trivillian *eighteenth century*
Chawton, Hants Loewenthal *eighteenth, nineteenth century*
Hurley, Berks M Thomas *antique harpsichords, organs*

Southern England

There is a new antique shop in the delightful village of Winterbourne Dauntsey near Salisbury in Wiltshire. Here *Mrs Lavinia Thorpe* literally lives amongst her stock. At my last visit she had some fine pieces of furniture for sale in this elegant Georgian Manor House which is her home as well as her trading premises. Some smaller items are also housed in an outdoor showroom next to the main house. Ring the bell here first, it's much less awe-inspiring than the front door of The Manor House which looks as though it might be opened by a liveried flunky, and it's blocked up anyway!

32 Newly installed from Abdingdon are *Roger and Francesca Wilson*, 'newly' inasmuch as anything that's happened within three years in the antique business is new. They are now in *The Old George* Middle Wallop, Hants where there are several showrooms of furniture and decorative items, with the accent on oak pieces.

The *Paddock Antiques* in Blandford, Dorset, occupy premises built in the fifteenth century. In the ground and upper floor showrooms the emphasis is on Georgian pieces of English furniture though earlier oak is often to be found. Next to Jane Austen's house at Chawton near Alton, Hants you will find Clinkers Antiques. Early oak is the mainstay of an interesting and varied stock displayed throughout seven showrooms. Besides the early oak there are some reasonably priced and useful eighteenth century pieces for the country house or cottage. In the gallery upstairs there is some good walnut, William and Mary and Queen Anne furniture. One thing that always strikes me on visiting Clinkers Antiques is the excellent polish and appearance of the stock. Enterprising young proprietors, *Mr and Mrs Robin Thomson*, attribute this to being good polishers and the shop always has that lovely lingering aroma of newly polished wood.

E W J Legg has been established in Dorchester, Dorset, for many years. There is a much larger stock of pre-1830 antiques to be seen than a casual glance in the window at Regency House, High St East, may indicate. Always pleased to do business with the trade and equally delighted to greet the private collector there is, in consequence, a wide stock to suit all tastes.

For four generations the name of *Spicer* has been known to serious collectors of antiques on both sides of the Atlantic. Many Americans in search of antiques make one of their first calls in Britain at Ivy Spicer's corner house conveniently situated on the main road from Southampton and Bournemouth on the outskirts of Winchester, Hants. (The house is called Redruth, 96 Cross St). Among the old English and continental furniture the caller will undoubtedly find something to prize among this general stock of quality antiques.

At Jewry St in the city itself, *J W Blanchard's* showrooms are as fascinating as his stock. Once the city's historic Debtor's Prison, *Mr Blanchard's* showrooms are now full of antiques. The gaol has become a goal for collectors. This is one of the largest and most comprehensive stocks of antique furniture in the south. Although difficult to come by these days, breakfront bookcases are a speciality.

The next port-of-call in Winchester has to be the beautiful Cathedral, perhaps immortalised for the young recently in the pop song of the same name. Recently threatened with subsidence when it was discovered to be literally floating on a marsh, thousands of tons of concrete have been pumped into the foundations to stablise this architectural monument.

Go out of Cathedral Square and down through the town to the delightful premises of *Mr and Mrs Behrens* on the corner of Chesil and Bridge Streets. Some very nice furniture here. Turn right into Chesil Street to visit *H J Viney & Daughter Ltd* who are specialists in antique mahogany and walnut furniture.

Oast houses are pretty things even when used for their proper purpose which is to dry hops, but they lend themselves even more prettily to conversion and use as an antique showrooms. A fantastic stock of stripped pine is offered for retail sale only in

Exquisite panelling from the extensive stock at Crowther of Syon Lodge, Isleworth, Middlesex

such premises by *Vercasson Ltd*, at Icklesham in Sussex. Just out-side the famous village of Winchelsea on the Hastings Road (A259) you turn left at The Robin Hood Inn. Wind down Water-mill Lane for a mile or so, and you will see Old Oast Place set behind a large pond. *Mr and Mrs Williams* live on the premises and can be contacted out of hours by appointment. This stock is really worth visiting, and polaroid pictures of individual pieces will be sent on request.

An entirely different type of stock, but in equally beautiful premises is *Peel Barton Antiques* at Curry Rivel near Langport, Somerset. The setting is breath-taking, especially in summer. But please don't take a trip just to gawp at the flowers, it's terribly irritating for the owners. *Major and Mrs Cater* have four showrooms of antique furniture and other small items such as porcelain and silver. The accent is on high quality walnut, but there is excellent oak and, of course, mahogany. Peel Barton Antiques can be found on the A378 Ilminster to Taunton road.

Some other dealers in southern England

Brighton, Sussex Trevor Antiques
Chichester, Sussex N Payne, Zene Walker
East Hoathley, Sussex W A Sloane *oak and Renaissance*
Lewes, Sussex S Moore Ltd
Liss, Hants D Clark *pine*
Midhurst, Sussex J Keil
Petworth, Sussex C Denman *oak*

Robertsbridge, Sussex P Westbury *oak*
Salisbury, Wilts Joiners Hall *seventeenth, eighteenth, nineteenth centuries*
Uckfield, Sussex Red Tiles *eighteenth century, Regency*
Wimborne Minster, Dorset Metcalfe Jackson
Winchester, Hants Brooks of Winchester *pine*, P King *oak*

Wales and the west country

It's always easy to find large stocks to recommend from import-ant dealers, it's more difficult to find small select shops with a few high quality items. One such business is *Jean Jones Antiques* of Taunton, Somerset. The shop has the atmosphere of an antique boutique. Small, elegant and tastefully laid out. Perhaps not more than a dozen pieces of furniture, but all excellent speci-mens such as a lovely George II walnut desk at my last visit. The furniture is prettily decorated with small items of silver and porcelain.

35

The most delightful Queen Anne house provides the setting for a large selection of important furniture. *Mr and Mrs Hall* offer a vast stock of high quality at Court House, Ash Priors near Bishops Lydeard, Taunton. At my last visit the selection ranged from Dutch marquetry to Victorian mahogany, running the gamut of walnut, oak and pine on the way. The house is currently being re-converted back to its original condition and the eventual effect will be a seven showroom mansion with one of the most important stocks in the west country.

Antique furniture always looks more inviting and homely if it is put into a room-setting rather than a showroom atmosphere. *F E Anderson* of Welshpool certainly believe in this philosophy and their display is always interspersed with beautiful flower arrangements such as you might have in your own home. The shop is opposite the Pheasant Inn and Britannia Passage, and the stock is varied with some fine oak pieces. A large painted wagon outside on the pavement marks the showroom of *Rocking Horse Antiques*, Llanfair Caereinion near Welshpool. A small, but nice stock of mainly oak pieces.

If you've never been to Portmeirion, you have to find a way to fit it in sometime. The whole set-up is enchanting and remarkable for its architectural achievement. Unbelievably a whole Italian village has been reconstructed on the Welsh coast, backed with magnificent woodland and bounded by the longest stretch of white sand I have seen in Wales. The buildings are truly characteristic – unlike other such attempts to bring the architectural idiosyncracies of another country across the sea, which so often look strangely bizarre and undeniably fake. Portmeirion has quite the opposite effect. The project really comes off and you can feel yourself in an old Italian village with the houses close together, painted white, pink and blue, typically decorated with plaques of the Madonna and child. The finest time of the year is late May and June when the rhododendrons have to be seen to be believed. Right in the heart of this quaint village is *Angel Antiques*. Two small showrooms, with small pieces of good furniture and a lot of pottery and porcelain.

It is extremely difficult for an antique dealer to have something of everything yet ruthlessly maintain a high standard of quality furniture. Such a business is *John Collins* of Bideford, Devon. Right in amongst plated egg-cup sets and fire irons there is usually some extremely fine furniture. At my last visit I saw an important table gibier and Louis Quinze cheval mirror. At number 63 High and also in a showroom opposite Mr Collins will deliver any quantity of goods purchased for about £1. As well as eighteenth century English and continental pieces, there is a showroom upstairs of a wide range of oak furniture.

Crispins Antiques in the small town of Dulverton, Somerset on the edge of Exmoor has four showrooms of general antiques with some choice collectors' items. Visitors are encouraged to browse and appointments can be made outside normal business hours. The trade is always welcome.

Forde House situated on the Torquay Rd out of Newton Abbot, Devon was built in 1610 and was visited by William of Orange and King Charles I. Today callers at this fine seventeenth century mansion are collectors, for here is a large stock of country furniture, particularly oak and pine. Ten showrooms, many with period oak panelling and fine moulded ceilings include mahogany furniture, china, glass, pictures and general antiques.

J Morland Coon Ltd deal only in antiques. This is a principle rigidly adhered to by this firm who have been merchants to the trade for half a century with a sound retail business. The firm's showrooms and stores cover an area 12,000 square feet at Townsend Hill along the main Tavistock road on the outskirts of Plymouth, Devon. A large and varied stock consists of sixteenth, seventeenth and eighteenth century furniture, porcelain, pottery etc. Apart from buying for his business Mr Roger Morland Coon, as a Fellow of the Valuers Institute, spends a great deal of time in the valuation of antiques and works of art throughout the west country.

Royal Well Place is only a few minutes walk from the gracious promenade which is the epitome of Cheltenham, Glos. Here *Mary Packham* has a shop that caters, in particular, for young people encouraged by both Mrs Packham and her prices.

The old-established family business of *A T Philp & Son* in Cardiff, Glamorgan, offers a comprehensive stock at 77 Kimberley Rd. Good quality furniture is priced to appeal to the home-maker, and a few unusual collector's pieces are also usually to be found here. The firm's activities are directed by Peter Philp, well known writer, broadcaster and speaker. Mr Philp is a regular feature writer for *The Antique Finder* magazine and responsible for the potted history of furniture which introduced this chapter.

Gilbert Morris has been in the antiques trade for sixty years. Now with showrooms at Ffynnongroew, Carnaervon and nearby Mostyn he has taken his son into partnership, and maintains perhaps the largest stock of antiques in North Wales. Mr Morris began business with his father at Royton, Lancs at the beginning of the century. The first antique he ever bought was a Chippendale partners desk from a local mill owner. 'I paid 25*s* for it,' he told me. 'It would easily fetch £250 today. In those days I was buying spindle back chairs in Oldham for half-a-crown apiece. A set of six two-arm ladder-back chairs were sold for £3 10*s* . . .' Welsh dressers are a speciality of the North Wales Antiques Galleries. Mr Morris drives many, many hundreds of miles over the years buying them. 'During the 1920's,' he recalls, 'I could buy as many as I wanted in Swansea, Cardiff, and Aberystwyth for £4 10*s* each. Now I am lucky to find a good one for £50–£60.'

More than fifty years of antique dealing have brought trade respect and collectors from all over the world to the Boringdon Villas premises of Reg and Muriel Andrade Ltd. Now, at number three Boringdon Villas their son, Mr Philip Andrade

One of Mr Thornton's showrooms at Faringdon Galleries, Berkshire. Mr Thornton speaks five languages; his quality stock is always modestly priced

brings the same flair to his fine selection of quality furniture. All the showrooms are tastefully arranged, with rare pieces shown to perfection, and complemented by a few good oil paintings together with ormulu and bronze ornaments. This is one of the best stocks in the West of England.

Some other dealers in Wales and the west country

Aberystwyth, Cards White
welsh dressers
Bath, Som C Angell,
M Sainsbury
Birdlip, nr Gloucester
F Norden *oak*
Broadway, Worcs M Brett
eighteenth century, H W Keil
eighteenth century, The Top Shop
oak
Cheltenham, Glos H W Keil
eighteenth century
Chudleigh, Devon R Martin

Frome, Som Keyford Galleries
Gillingham, Dorset Harwood
House
Honiton, Devon G N Butler,
Rummery Antiques
Kingsbridge, Devon Halsey
Malmesbury, Wilts F Dryden
Moreton-in-the-Marsh, Worcs
G Bolam *eighteenth century*
Plymouth, Devon Island House
Ruthin, Denbighs Grosvenor
Galleries *welsh dressers*
Wincanton, Som G Olive

Midlands and the north

No review of fine furniture dealers would be complete without a capital letter mention for Chester. Here there are three quite outstanding shops, *The Olde Leche House* 21 Watergate Row, *Quinney's* of 49–61 Bridge St and *Wellesley Wilson* of 29 Watergate Row. All these dealers offer an outstanding range of fine quality seventeenth, eighteenth and Regency furniture.

While driving through the Derbyshire dales I came across a very fine stock of furniture of all periods at Swiss House, Castleton near Sheffield. A fine painted French boudoir suite was on display at our last visit but *John Kelsey* has further showrooms upstairs, and an enormous converted dance hall next door which houses Edwardian and Victorian items.

More and more young people are discovering pine as an inexpensive way of indulging their love of antiques and of brightening up a house or flat. At Alderley Edge in Cheshire, *Shirley Eaton* has a lot of stripped pine, especially chests of drawers.

Coming out of the delightful town of Knutsford and going towards Buxton you will pass the premises of *John Duxfield Antiques*. The window may belie the fact that there is a good stock of furniture which extends into three further showrooms which you cannot see from the road. If you get lost, ask for 15 Brook St.

There is a fine selection of furniture and decorative pieces at *G W Ford and Son* of Glossop Rd, Sheffield. I saw several sets of dining chairs and a choice of three mahogany tables at my last visit. These items, being so hard to find these days, it shows that Mr and Mrs Ford are really on the ball when it comes to knowing what their customers want. Mr Ford is helpful to the private buyer and gives customers a useful ready reckoner of dates to help them understand the exact period of furniture which may described as Queen Anne or George II on the ticket. There are three showrooms on the ground floor, but ask to see the old cellar also where there is a showroom for oak and less important pieces.

W Mellows is to be found at Brereton Hall, a couple of miles to the south of Rugeley on the A51 Lichfield Rd. This large Queen Anne house with a later Georgian facade contains two showrooms which lend themselves ideally to a stock of quality eighteenth century furniture.

Withers of Leicester was established in 1860 and with the fourth generation of the family in the business this firm still flourishes at fairly recently acquired premises near Victoria Park. There are three floors of showrooms containing a varied stock. The accent is on eighteenth and nineteenth century English and continental furniture of fine quality, also smaller items.

In Shrewsbury, Salop, High St under the sign of an old painted tobacconist's figure *Walter Wycherley* and his nephew, Richard, carry on the family business founded in the town in 1813. Walter Wycherley has been in the business for 55 years joining in 1908 as an apprentice cabinet maker and carver under his father. The late Queen Mary was a constant caller at the firm's shop when in the 1920's her brother and sister-in-law the Duke and Duchess of Cambridge, lived at nearby Shotton Hall. Mr Wycherley has seen many changes over the years. The county trade has given over to a demand for smaller furniture. A wide range of high standard is always in stock.

Another large stock can be found in Birmingham offered by *James Reeve* at 11 Cumberland St. Established more than a century James Reeve has one of the largest stocks in the Midlands. Nearby in Solihull are the premises of *A T Silvester & Sons*.

Again a large stock of mainly eighteenth century and Regency furniture at their Warwick Rd address, and a new showroom for oak furniture at The Old House Knowle which is on the main A41 to Warwick. More furniture from the same company can be found at 2 and 4 High St, Warwick. Not far away, at Vesey Manor, Sutton Coldfield, *Thomas Coulborn* specialises in seventeenth and eighteenth century English furniture.

R Greenwood of Haslingden, Lancs, shows an impressive collection of antique oak furniture. Welsh, Shropshire, Lancashire and Yorkshire dressers are inevitably to be found along with gate-leg and other tables, windsor, ladder and spindle-back chairs.

There were antiques piled from floor to ceiling at the West End Galleries, Buxton, Derby. It is not surprising, therefore, that antique dealers from abroad call here to see *Messrs Hockenhull and Needham*. Eighteenth century continental furniture is a feature of the stock but the policy, too, is to have as much a mixture as possible so that no one goes away disappointed. Two doors away E Hockenhull maintains a stock of general antiques with a section devoted to oak, in which anyone interested in acquiring an oak dresser would do well to look, as Mr Hockenhull has a long-standing reputation in the north for finding these sought-after pieces.

Some of the finest examples of eighteenth century English furniture can always be found in *Walter Waddingham's* showrooms in Harrogate, Yorks, across the road from the Old Spa Pump Room. This is one of the most important calls for the collector in the north.

William Spinks, E Waller and *Bell & Edmondson* of Kendal, Westmorland all offer a selection of nice furniture. So if you're visiting the Lake district you should go to Kendal on a shopping spree. Also in Kendal is *Richard Phillips* who has recently moved to larger premises on Mawky Hill, named so he says, 'because Kendalians find this easier to pronounce than Malt Kiln Hill'.

Edinburgh has charm and its antique shops have character. Through cobbled streets, spacious squares and broad thoroughfares the collector can spend many hours going from dealer to dealer. *Alexander Adamson* in association with *A Ross Farrow* specialises in eighteenth century furniture, porcelain and silver. Scottish antiques are to be found in a shop at Melbourne Place, Edinburgh run by enterprising *Peter Nicholson*. **41**

Aberdeen, the granite city, probably offers the largest stock of antiques under one roof in Scotland at *John Bell*. A vast stock spreads through six floors and numerous showrooms. And the many who write in each day with requests always receive a reply by return. In both cases you can rely on personal attention from Mr W S Bell who began business in Aberdeen as a boy and has built up one of the most famous antique businesses in the world.

At Bakewell in Derbyshire, *Maurice Goldstone* has 22 showrooms where he specialises in early oak furniture. Rivalling *Mary Bellis* of Hungerford, Mr Goldstone claims the most important stock in the country, and displayed most beautifully in mediaeval and Tudor Buildings.

At 10 Church St, Ludlow, Salop and Tamberlane House, *Mr and Mrs Paul Smith* present a wide range of antique furniture. The accent is on Georgian mahogany and rosewood, with earlier oak, yew and walnut in a comprehensive stock that naturally includes paintings, clocks, barometers and the like.

Some other dealers in the midlands and the north

Aberdeen, Scotland W Young
Accrington, Lancs Graveson
Bakewell, Derbys
M Goldstone *oak*
Birmingham, Warks J Reeve
Burley-in-Wharfdale, Yorks
Sylvia Head
Edinburgh, Scotland P Couts
Harrogate, Yorks The Attic
pine, C Lumb, Waddingham
eighteenth century
Ilkeley, Yorks Cooper & Son
oak, eighteenth century
Loughborough, Leics Lowe of
Loughborough Ltd *eighteenth,
nineteenth century*

Manchester, Lancs
The Connoisseur *French furniture*
Northampton, Northants
J Roberts
Otley, Yorks Suttle *oak*
**Paulerspury, nr Towcester,
Northants** Malcolm Cameron
Antique Galleries
Penrith, Westmorland
H Kirsop *oak*
Pershore, Worcs Mercy Jeboult
Preston, Lancs F Treasure
Skipton, Yorks Myers Galleries
special oak room
Stamford, Lincs Scotney &
Son *seventeenth, eighteenth century*

East Anglia

Mr & Mrs D Lewellen's shop in Bungay, has a larger stock of antiques than one hopes to find in this small Suffolk town. Among a large selection of small decorative items there is a good stock of furniture at 28 and 30 Earsham St.

At 25 Bridge St, Cambridge, built when the first Queen

*Mr Charles Morse of Earls Colne deals in 16th and 17th century
English and Continental oak furniture and early oil paintings*

Elizabeth was on the throne, one can talk about antiques to
Walter Stockbridge, an antique dealer in Cambridge since joining
the family business as a sixteen-year-old. Mr Stockbridge began
his career by working for five years at the bench as a cabinet
maker. 'The only royal road to judgement of furniture is to know
the construction and how the eighteenth century cabinet makers
worked'. W Stockbridge & Sons Ltd, established in 1870, **43**

specializes in fine eighteenth century furniture with a particularly good selection of mahogany and walnut.

Wilfred Bull always seems to have numerous and particularly fine examples of eighteenth century English and continental furniture in his shop in Coggeshall, Essex. Should one find the door closed, a notice directs you to Mr Bull's extensive showrooms, just around the corner in Kelvedon Rd, where there is always someone to extend a welcome and assist you. These showrooms contain a large and comprehensive selection of fine furniture. On the main road from East Anglia to London, halfway between Harlow and Epping, is Rundells Antiques. Here you enter a large showroom through a courtyard – once the headquarters of the Essex hunt. Both in a barn and the adjacent large Queen Anne house, where *Mr & Mrs Cox* are always ready to meet collectors from abroad, there is a large stock of general antiques with the accent on mahogany furniture.

At *Manor Antiques*, 43 Hoddesdon Rd, St Margarets there is an enormous barn showroom filled to the ceiling with pine, oak and country items. At White Colne near Colchester, *Compton-Dando* has several showrooms of fine eighteenth century and Regency pieces, as well as a converted coach-house full of country items.

In ancient Norwich, Norfolk one expects to see fine antique furniture, and *Arthur Brett & Sons* does not disappoint. A really comprehensive stock of good English antique furniture is displayed in a Georgian house, the main rooms retaining their original panelling. The collector and those wishing to furnish a complete room are equally well catered for.

An Old Coaching House is the apt showroom for an important stock of early oak furniture at The White House, Earls Colne, Essex. *Charles Morse* an ex-journalist, always has a comprehensive selection of English pieces and French provincial furniture is usually represented. A keen art lover, Mr Morse also offers fine paintings, mainly sixteenth and seventeenth century, together with some early sculpture and antiquities.

Some other dealers in East Anglia

Burnham Market, Norfolk
Trimmers *closed Tuesday*
Cambridge J Beazor,

M Clark, S Woolston
Cromer, Norfolk Cromer
Antique Gallery
Earls Colne, Essex

Compton-Dando
Gt Yarmouth, Norfolk
P Howkins
Norwich, Norfolk Rackheath

Hall, H Levine, H Beazor,
A Brett, Paston House
South Walsham, Norfolk
The Old Curiosity Shop

Furniture restoration and reproduction

It is not unusual that the case presents itself where you may have four perfect antique chairs, and spend ten hapless years trying to match up the other two to get a set of six dining chairs. There is no reason at all why in the interim you should not have the original chairs copied so that you have a serviceable set and can look at your leisure for the right pieces.

E M F Brown Ltd Church Lane, High St, West Wycombe, Bucks specialise in hand-made period chairs, English and French, also repairs and restoration work. They will cane or rush the seats and undertake to copy period chairs in any wood. They also offer a reproduction service for four poster beds, pedestal tables, veneered cabinets – or almost anything you should require. An illustrated catalogue of period English chairs is available on request.

Some restorers of antique furniture

Maurice Antiques, 202 Brecknock Rd, Tufnell Park, London N19, 607 2371
P Boswell (Restorations) Ltd, 67 Beak St, London W1, 734 6543
Fernandes & Marche, 80 Islington High St, London N1, 837 8768
R Newton, 576 Kings Rd, London SW6, 736 1804
J Taylor, 168 Marlborough Rd, London N19, 272 8462
G Watford, 246 Haydons' Rd, London SW19, 540 2237 *chair caning*
E & A Wates Ltd, 82 Mitcham Lane, London SW16, 769 2205
Cooper's of Ilkley, 33 Church St, Ilkley, Yorks, 42595
D J Down, 11 Tottenham Mews, London W1, 636 3464
C J Quinlan, 309 Fulham Rd, SW6, *chair caners*

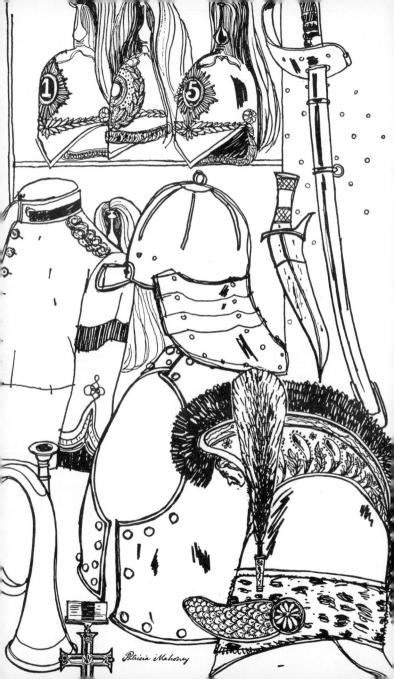

Patricia Mahoney

Chapter two

arms, armour and militaria

Demand is growing much faster than the supply in these fields. Take an example from the auction price review of the well-known specialist auctioneers *Wallis & Wallis* of Lewes. In January 1944 a pair of flintlock duelling pistols fetched £175 and at the end of the same season, December 1944 a similar pair realised £370. The price would now be between £1,500 and £2,000. The same price spiral can be noted by studying sale catalogues over the years and will be found to apply to all kinds of militaria from powder horns to Luftwaffe daggers.

The beginnings of the mania for collecting military objects often starts in childhood. Many a young boy has had endless fun spending his pocket money on regimental tunic buttons or miniature decorations. Indeed, some very important collections have sprung from such humble beginnings. And some items are still within the reach of the modest purse. Campaign medals for instance. Medals and decorations have a personal appeal since the name of the recipient is usually engraved around the edge or on the back of the piece concerned. With the more important orders, such as the DSO or MC, there may even be a published citation, giving a brief account of the deed which merited the award. Such citations can be found in *The London Gazette*, a copy of which may be consulted at most public libraries. For a really interesting find, a photostat copy of the citation can be purchased for about a shilling on application to Her Majesty's Stationery Office. The enthusiast will probably start by collecting general examples representative of the major military campaigns and then specialise in a period, such as the Crimean war. 47

Napoleonic relics, such as the Military General Service Medal issued in 1849 to survivors of the Peninsula wars of 1793–1814, are much sought after. The awards were a little tardy perhaps, but even recognition is better late than never! A set of three awards from the 1914–18 war, the 1914–15 Star, the British War Medal and the Victory Medal will cost only about £3, but if you aspire to owning a VC, however, be prepared for a bill between £1,000 and £2,000.

Campaign ribbons and miniature decorations are merely a matter of shillings, the former starting at about threepence an inch. These are ideal for getting the feel of the thing before investing more heavily.

Another interesting collectors' piece is the shoulder belt plate, an oval medallion bearing the regimental crest which was worn high on the shoulder belt and can be seen quite clearly in portraits of military gentlemen in full regalia. Similar items, now keenly sought are the sabretache and the gorget.

Playing model soldiers is still very much a game for grown-ups, for the serious militarist that is. There are shops which specialise in the sale of beautiful lead figurines, all hand-painted in the glorious colours of bygone regiments, on foot, on horse-back, encamped, entrenched, or even aboard ship. Prices start at about £6 (painted) according to the complexity of the figure or group. In order to play the game properly the enthusiast must subscribe to a war games magazine. For instance *Tradition* devotes a special section each issue to planning war games for its readers to play with their model armies. So that the casual reader shall not under-estimate the seriousness of such sport, let me quote from a past issue '. . . the two short-range projectiles, grapeshot and canister (the latter sometimes referred to as case shot) are best represented by pieces of wire bent into the shape of two isosceles triangles, measuring 250*mm* by 75*mm* and 125*mm* by 50*mm* respectively. The narrow pointed end is placed against the cannon mouth and figures touched or covered by the triangle indicating grapeshot are thrown for by two dice. In the case of canister, the heavier of the two and with greater stopping power, everything touched or inside the wire is presumed dead . . .'. Food for thought indeed! Copies of *Tradition* also carry full colour plates of regimental gear, with many fascinating and comprehensive articles on military subjects such as who wore what, when, and The battle of Waterloo. Copies cost

17s 6d each from Belmont-Maitland Publishers Ltd, 44 Dover St, London W1, but an annual subscription of £5 5s covers membership of *The International Society of Military Collectors*, which meets on the second Friday of the month in London.

Books to read

Firearms and weapons

The age of firearms R Held
Cassell 63s
**Antique firearms: their care,
repair, restoration** R Lister
Barrie 45s
The archaeology of weapons
E Oakeshott Lutterworth 45s
Armour and weapons
P Martin Barrie 105s
Arms and armour *Thomas,
Samber & Schedelmann* Thames
168s
Arms and armour
H Blackmore S Vista 10s 6d
**The art of the gunmaker
1500–1660** *J Hayward* Barrie 110s
**The art of the gunmaker
1660–1830** *J Hayward* Barrie 110s
**The art of the Japanese
sword** *B Robinson* Faber 63s
The book of the gun
H Peterson Hamlyn 39s 6d
British military firearms
H Blackmore Barrie 60s
The British soldier's firearm
C H Roads Barrie 75s

Collectors' guns *D Myrns* Arco
24s
Daggers & fighting knives
H Peterson Barrie 35s
Duelling pistols *J Atkinson*
Cassell 50s
Early percussion firearms
L Winant Barrie 55s
**The encyclopaedia of
firearms** Connoisseur 70s
European armour *C Blair*
Batsford 35s
**European and American
arms** *C Blair* Batsford 147s
**Firearm collecting for
amateurs** *J Henderson* Muller
18s
Firearms *H Blackmore* S Vista
8s 6d
Firearms *H Ricketts* Weidenfeld
30s
A history of firearms *Carmen*
Routledge 21s
Gun collecting *G Boothroyd* Arco
5s
Guns and rifles of the world 49

Model soldiers *H Harris*
Weidenfeld 30s
Orders, medals and decorations of England and Europe in colour *H Mussen*
Blandford 30s
A history of regiments and uniforms of the British army
R M Barnes Seeley Service 42s
Ribbons and medals *Dorling*
G Philip 25s
Uniforms and history of the Scottish regiments *R M Barnes*
Seeley Service 42s

A fine stock of bibliography on the subject of arms, armour and militaria is held by *Kenneth Trotman* 18 Manwell Rd, Swanage, Dorset. View by appointment only (Swanage 3985). Catalogues by request

world in colour *Kannik*
Blandford 30s
Model soldiers *Garratt*
Seeley Service 42s

Where to buy

Some dealers in London

W1/ M & J Appleby *guns, weapons, uniforms, militaria*
Corbitt & Hunter *medals*
E Fairclough *firearms, weapons, including oriental swords*

J H L Hayward *war medals, militaria, decorations*
Limner Antiques, Bond St
Antique Market *general militaria and weapons*

painting, ships models, weapons
B A Seaby *war medals and
decorations*
Tradition 188 Piccadilly
militaria, weapons, uniforms
W2/P C L German *arms and
armour*
D Young *militaria*
WC2/A H Baldwin & Sons
campaign medals and decorations
N1/Grejoron Antiques *weapons*
C Farlowes Militaria Vault,
Camden Passage *imperial and
nazi militaria*
SW1/P Dale *militaria, weapons,
armour and armorial devices,
including prints*

Some dealers in the home counties

Brenchley, Kent The Brenchley
Gallery *marine prints, naval
bygones, watercolours*
Canterbury, Kent Sun
Antiques *arms, armour, militaria*

Hatfield, Herts Grejoron
weapons
Reigate, Surrey J Powell
weapons and firearms
Richmond, Surrey Antiquaria
& Little Gallery *swords*

Some dealers in southern England

Bournemouth, Hants Capt R J
Tompkins *militaria*
Bridport, Dorset The Antique
Shop *small militaria*
Brighton, Sussex The Armoury
arms, armour, medals, Sterrys
firearms and weapons
Lindfield, Sussex A Thomas
arms and militaria
Portsmouth, Hants Ophir
Antiques *arms, armour*
Southsea, Hants Radford
Antiques *weapons*

Some dealers in Wales and the west country

Bristol Quinney's Antiques
firearms
Cheltenham, Glos J Kesterton
firearms, weapons, militaria
Clifton, nr Bristol Clifton
Galleries *firearms, armour*
Honiton, Devon J A Bryant
pistols
Newnham-on-Severn, Glos
Castle Antiques *arms, armour,*
G Kenyon-May *arms, armour,
marine bygones*
Ross-on-Wye, Hereford
Old Court House
Taunton, Som The Treasure
Chest *badges and small militaria*
Tetbury, Glos Two Toads
Antiques *weapons*

Torquay, Devon Silver Pixie
Truro, Cornwall The Antique
Shop *firearms, weapons, militaria*
Worcester Stirling-Brown
general militaria

Some dealers in the midlands and the north

Birmingham, Warks
The Format Coin & Metal Co
militaria
Briercliffe, nr Burnley, Lancs
H Sutcliffe *firearms, weapons*
Cheltenham, Glos J Kesterton
*arms, armour, shields, weapons,
medals*
Chester, Cheshire Collector's
Find *pistols*, Watergate Antiques
swords, pistols, militaria
Edinburgh, Scotland Nicholson
Antiques *swords, Scottish weapons*
Glasgow, Scotland Captain
A McAdam *weapons*, Muirhead
Moffat & Co *arms, armour*,
Nicholson Antiques *swords,
Scottish weapons*
Harrogate, Yorks Greenwood
weapons
Inverness, Scotland J F Kelly
Scottish weapons
Leicester, Leics J A Morrison
arms, armour, weapons, militaria
Manchester, Lancs
The Armourer's Shop *arms,
armour*
Mountsorrel, Leics J & M Mee
firearms
Newcastle, Northumberland
Corbitt & Hunter *medals*
Nottingham, Notts D Potter
swords
St Annes-on-Sea, Lancs
Spinning Wheel Antiques *arms,
militaria*

Stratford-upon-Avon, Warks
J Wigington *weapons, arms,
armour*, Poets Arbour

Some dealers in East Anglia

Clacton, Essex Pennyfarthing
Antiques *weapons, militaria*
Cley-next-the-Sea, Suffolk
Studio Antico *arms, armour*
Lavenham, Suffolk Staddles
Antiques *weapons, armour*
**Littlebury, Saffron Walden,
Essex** Old Carpenters Arms
general militaria and naval bygones
Saffron Walden, Essex
Walkyier *arms*

Some specialist auctioneers

Glendining & Co Ltd,
Blenstock House, 7 Blenheim St,
New Bond St, London W1,
499 8541, *about eight sales each year
of military and naval medals,
oriental armour*
Wallis & Wallis, 210 High St,
Lewes, Sussex, Lewes 3137, *nine
sales a year of arms, armour,
militaria, medals*
Weller & Dufty Ltd, The Fine
Art Salerooms, 141 Bromsgrove
St, Birmingham 5, Warwickshire,
021 692 1414/5, *nine two-day
auctions each year. Each sale averages
1,000 lots. Illustrated catalogues
on request (armour and arms)*

Restorer of antique guns

Norman's of Framlingham,
Church St, Framlingham,
Suffolk, Framlingham 500

53

Patricia Mahoney

Chapter three

pictures, prints and maps

This chapter covers oil paintings, water colours, gouaches, etchings, prints, engravings, and sculpture, to which must also be added maps because these are mostly handled by print and engraving specialists. The price range is enormous, varying from a few shillings for unframed book illustrations to a fortune for an old master. London dealers of international repute dealing in old masters have been listed separately from those where a permanent or varied stock of traditional works is to be found at prices suited to the more modest collector. There are still bargains to be found but also mistakes to be made. I once bought four signed coloured prints of birds by James Thorburn for ten shillings from a stall in Bethnal Green, London when their trade value was about five pounds each. I have also paid £20 for an oil painting that I hoped was of the sixteenth century Dutch school only to have it ruined by bad cleaning.

Take care to avoid being deceived by German lithographic prints of early oil paintings known as oleographs. Reproduced on canvas-type paper with prominent brush strokes suitably embossed they can often be mistaken for genuine oils. In some cases the oleograph is stuck on to a genuine old canvas, so when in doubt insist on removing the canvas from its frame and look for the tell-tale edge of the print usually to be found on the return of the stretcher-board or, sometimes, when they are stuck onto a wooden panel, on the reverse side. I have even known an over-eager professional give several pounds for such a panel, heavily varnished, and suitably aged in appearance.

Do not confuse reproductions with copies. Copies of old masters **55** and for that matter of any artist whose work commands a reasonable figure, abound. Copies are not necessarily a bad buy if they are well executed. They may have been painted by a member or apprentice of the school of the painter of the original work in which case they would probably not have been allowed to leave the studio without the master's approval or even a few deft finishing strokes from his own brush. These contemporary copies or school paintings often command high prices in their own right. On the other hand, one has only to visit some of the better known international galleries on the appropriate days and watch the teenage art students laboriously imitating well known works stroke by stroke, to realise that there is an enormous number of modern and indifferent copies in circulation because, however talented these young artists are, their work lacks the guidance of the original master.

Remember this tip: the picture is often older than the frame but seldom is the frame older than the picture – except maybe in the case of a deliberate high-priced fake, and the serious collector of oil paintings would do well to study frames. To give an example, I was able to identify a so-called copy portrait of Sir John Dryden the first poet laureate (circa 1680) because it was framed in a genuine hand carved laurel-wreath frame of the period, obviously purposely made for the subject. On the cleaning the portrait, experts agreed that it was the work of Sir Godfrey Kneller. In this case its provenance was easy to establish because it had remained in the family who had regarded it as a worthless copy because a similar portrait which graced the walls of a University was considered to be the original. Now I happen to know a painter who often painted several portraits of a well-known sitter commissioned to paint one for an institution or guild. Invariably the sitter's family acquired one of the duplicate portraits. From the quality of the painting I surmised that this was probably the case with the Dryden portrait, but it was the frame which gave the clue. To identify frames read *The Art and history of frames* by Henry Heydenryke (Nicholas Vane).

For the more modest collector good prints, etchings, and old maps provide a much wider field of selection. The more expensive and rare are those prints engraved, etched or lithographed by the artist himself. More common are those where the print has been engraved by an artist or craftsman from the original work of another. The British Museum and The Victoria and

Albert Museum have fine collections of all types of etchings, engravings, lithographs and mezzotints, and provincial museums nearly always have a selection by local artists. Many charming prints of historic views, flowers and birds are to be found in second-hand book shops because most prints of this nature were originally book illustrations and sometimes can be picked up very cheaply – from a few shillings upwards.

Books to read

Arabian miniatures *Murray* 21s
Art collecting for amateurs
R Seddon Muller 21s
Art nouveau *M Amaya* Studio
Vista 12s 6d
Art through the ages
H Gardner Bell 60s
The arts of China
H Munsterberg Tuttle 127s
The arts of Japan
H Munsterberg Tuttle 35s
British painting *J Woodward*
Studio Vista 21s
British portrait miniatures
D Foskett Spring 35s
British portrait miniatures
D Foskett Methuen 105s
British silhouettes
J Woodiwiss Country Life 50s
A concise history of bronzes
G Savage Thames 35s
A handbook of Chinese art

M Medley Bell 22s 6d
A short history of Chinese art
M Sullivan Faber 21s
**Christian and Byzantine
painting** *Graber and Chatzidakis*
Weidenfeld 12s 6d
Classical school of Japan
O Holloway Tiranti 30s
The cleaning of paintings
H Ruhemann Faber 126s
Constable oil sketches
J Baskett Barrie 105s
Decorative printed maps
R Skelton Spring 35s
**A dictionary of Victorian
landscape painters** *G Reynolds*
Studio Vista 105s
Early Christian painting
De Bourguet Weidenfeld 12s 6d
Early Venetian painters
F Godfrey Tiranti 9s
18th century painting

One small corner of the extensive showrooms at Gomshall Gallery in Surrey. A fine selection of nautical paintings is always available

F Russoli Weidenfeld 12s 6d
The rise and fall of picture prices 1760–1960 *G Reitlinger* 50s
Roman Etruscan painting *A Stenico* Weidenfeld 12s 6d
Romanesque painting *J Ainaud* Weidenfeld 12s 6d
Seventeenth century painting *F Cogniat* Weidenfeld 12s 6d
Silhouettes *P Hickman* Jenkins 32s

Turner watercolours *M Butlin* Barrie 105s
Twentieth century painting *H Jaffe* Weidenfeld 12s 6d
Victorian painters *J Maas* Barrie 126s
Victorian painting *G Reynolds* Studio Vista 105s
Watercolour painting in Britain (3 vols) *M Hardie* Batsford 126s

Public Galleries to visit

London

British Museum Gt Russell St, WC1 *prints, drawings, manuscripts*
Buckingham Palace The Queens Gallery, Buckingham Palace Rd, SW1
Carlyle's House 24 Cheyne Row, SW3 *portraits, prints, manuscripts*
Dicken's House 48 Doughty St, WC1 *portraits, manuscripts*
Dulwich College Picture Gallery College Rd, SE21 *Spanish and Dutch*
Grabowski Gallery 84, Sloane Ave, SW3 *English and Polish*
Hogarth's House Hogarth Lane, Chiswick W4 *Hogarth paintings*
The Iveagh Bequest Kenwood, NW3 *Rembrandt, Vermeer, Van Dyck etc*
Keats House and Museum Keats Grove, NW3 *manuscripts*
National Gallery Trafalgar Square, WC2 *English and European paintings of all schools*
National Portrait Gallery St Martin's Place, Trafalgar Sq, WC2
National Maritime Museum Romney Rd, Greenwich, SE10 *maritime interest*
Tate Gallery Millbank SW1 *paintings and sculpture*
Wallace Collection Hertford House, Manchester Square, W1 *miniatures, sculpture, paintings of English and European schools*
Wellington Museum Apsley

House, Hyde Park Corner, W1
paintings

Home counties and south

Bembridge, Isle of Wight
The Ruskin Gallery, Bembridge
School

Bournemouth, Hants The
Russel Cotes Art Gallery,
East Cliff

Brighton, Sussex Brighton Art
Gallery, Church St

Portsmouth, Hants The
Victory Museum, HM Dockyard
marine interest

Southampton, Hants
Southampton Art Gallery,
Civic Centre

Wales and the west

Aberystwyth, Cardigan
The National Library of Wales

Bath, Somerset Victoria Art
Gallery, Bridge St

Bristol, Somerset City Art
Gallery, Queens Rd

Llandudno, Caernarvon
Rapallo House Museum and
Art Gallery, Fferm Bach
Craig-y-Don

South and north midlands, north and Scotland

Aberdeen Aberdeen Art Gallery
and Museum, School Hill

Barnard Castle, Durham
The Bowes Museum

Birkenhead, Cheshire
Williamson Art Gallery, Slate Rd

Birmingham, Warks
City Museum and Art Gallery,
Congreve St

Bolton, Lancs Museum and Art
Gallery, Lyon St School

60 Bradford, Yorks City Art
Gallery, Cartwright memorial
Hall

Brighouse, Yorks Brighouse
Art Gallery, Halifax Rd

Dundee, Angus Orchar Art
Gallery, Broughty Ferry
Whistler etchings

Edinburgh National Gallery of
Scotland, The Mound,
Edinburgh 1

Edinburgh Scottish National
Gallery, Queen St, Edinburgh 2

Glasgow Art Gallery and
Museum, Kelvingrove

Leamington Spa, Warks
Leamington Spa Art Gallery and
Museum, Avenue Rd

Leeds, Yorks City Art Gallery

Liverpool, Lancs Walker Art
Gallery, William Brown St

Liverpool, Lancs Sudley Art
Gallery and Museum, Mossley
Hill Rd

Manchester, Lancs The City
Art Gallery, Mosley St

Manchester, Lancs Whitworth
Art Gallery, Oxford Rd

**Newcastle-upon-Tyne,
Northumberland** Laing Art
Gallery and Museum, Gham
Place

**Newcastle-upon-Tyne,
Northumberland** The Hatton
Gallery, University of Newcastle

Nottingham, Notts City
Museum and Art Gallery,
The Castle

Oldham, Lancs Municipal Art
Gallery, Union St

Sheffield, Yorks Graves Art
Gallery, Surrey St

Wolverhampton Municipal Art
Gallery, Lichfield St

York City of York Art Gallery,
Exhibition Square

Where to buy

Some picture and print dealers in London

W1/A Ackerman & Son Ltd *paintings, sporting prints*

T Agnew & Sons Ltd *all schools*

Arcade Gallery Ltd *Baroque paintings, sculpture from Asia, Africa*

P & D Colnagho & Co Ltd *seventeenth, eighteenth century Italian*

J G Couper (Fine Arts) Ltd *French nineteenth century*

W Drown *English, Dutch, Flemish, Italian masters*

Fine Art Society Ltd *English watercolours*

The Folio Society *drawings, prints, maps, antiquities*

Fores Ltd *nineteenth century English sporting*

Frost & Reed Ltd *all schools*

R Green *marine, sporting, land-scapes, flower and still life*

Hallsborough Gallery *all schools*

A Kauffman *all schools*

Lefevre Gallery *nineteenth, twentieth century French*

The Leger Galleries Ltd *all schools*

Leicester Galleries *nineteenth, twentieth century paintings and sculpture*

Lotinga Ltd *French nineteenth, twentieth century*

Manning Galleries Ltd *English, continental drawings*

Marlborough Fine Art Ltd *nineteenth, twentieth century all schools*

J Mitchell & Son *English, Dutch, Flemish*

Moorland Gallery, *sporting, natural history paintings*

Obelisk Gallery *oriental antiquities*

O'Hana Gallery *Impressionist*

Old Masters Galleries *European oils*

Parker Galleries *military, naval, sporting pictures*

F Partridge & Sons Ltd

61

eighteenth century English sporting
Patterson & Shipman Ltd *Dutch*
Roland, Browse & Delbanco
nineteenth, twentieth century French
Sabin Galleries *Dutch, Flemish*
E Speelman Ltd *all schools*
A G Tite *miniatures*
A Tooth & Sons Ltd *all schools*
Tyron Gallery *sporting, natural history*
Wildenstein & Co Ltd *all schools*
W2/H N Bier *drawings*
W8/B Bivall *seventeenth, eighteenth century oils*
R Cook Gallery *old master paintings, all schools*
Jeudwine *old master drawings pre-1800*
Pulitzer Gallery *old master drawings and watercolours*
W11/Caelt Gallery *all schools and periods*
W14/Schidlof Galleries *drawings, miniatures*
NW3/L Franklyn *Continental old master drawings, paintings*
H Jacobs *oils and watercolours eighteenth, nineteenth century*
SW1/Albany Gallery
Appleby Brothers *all schools*
M Bernard *eighteenth, nineteenth century English*
Brod Gallery *Dutch seventeenth century*
Bury Art Galleries *English watercolours*
Duits Ltd *seventeenth century Dutch, Flemish*
Ferrers *eighteenth, nineteenth*

century French
R Frank *Victorian*
Gallery Lasson *old masters*
Gooden & Fox Ltd *eighteenth century English*
Hazlitt Gallery *Italian, French*
Heim Gallery *old masters, sculpture*
Holbein Galleries *old masters*
Johnson, Oscar & Peter Ltd *eighteenth, nineteenth century English*
Kaplan Gallery *post-impressionist*
Knoedler & Co Ltd *Dutch,*

London as she was in 1574. A decorative copper plate engraving from Baynton-Williams, London SW7

62

Flemish
Koetser Gallery *Dutch, Flemish*
L Koetser *Dutch, Flemish, Italian*
P Larsen *old masters*
Leggatt Brothers *English*
MacConnal, Mason & Son
Continental, English paintings and drawings
J MacMaster *prints, engravings*
Mason Gallery *English, Dutch*
Newman *nineteenth century*
Omell Galleries *Scandinavian pictures*

Hal O'Nians *old masters*
Pawsey & Payne *English paintings, drawings*
R Preston *seascapes*
Sifton, Praed & Company *maps*
Marshall Spink Ltd *Dutch, Flemish*
Sutch & Martin *old masters*
D Vandekar *nineteenth century, Dutch, Flemish*
SW3/Maltzahn Gallery *old masters*
Quangle Prints *London*

topographic prints, nineteenth century
etching especially Whistler
Rutland Gallery *English
eighteenth, nineteenth century marine
and sporting*
Temple Gallery *Greek and Russian
icons, Indian, Persian miniatures*
SW7/Baynton-Williams *old maps
and prints*
SW10/W Ware Gallery *Dutch,
English*
SW13/Abbott and Holder
*watercolours and drawings in private
house*
WC1/Craddock & Barnard
etchings, prints, woodcuts
WC2/A Reader *sporting, military
and marine maps, prints*
EC2/City Gallery (landscape
paintings) 11–4 pm Mon–Fri

Some other dealers in the home counties

Amersham, Bucks Collectors
Treasures *maps and prints*
Brenchley, Kent The Brenchley
Gallery *marine watercolours and
prints*
Cambridge G Cozza *sporting
prints and maps*
E Hilton *general*
Cryershill, Bucks Sladmore
Antique Gallery *French nineteenth
century animal bronzes*
Dunstable, Beds Blaise Preston
Ltd *old masters, nineteenth century*
Farnham, Surrey T & H
Venables *military, sporting, naval
subjects*
Godalming, Surrey Stevens &
Brown *prints, drawings, book
illustrations*
Gomshall, nr Shere, Surrey
Vera Lloyd Galleries *marine,*

general oils
Guildford, Surrey C Traylen
maps, prints and manuscripts
Hawkhurst, Kent G B Lowe
prints
Harpenden, Herts
Hammersley Galleries *all schools,
by appt only*
Hertford L Partridge *prints,
paintings*
Marlow, Bucks Regency House
oil paintings
Oxford Bonfigioli Gallery
watercolours, sculpture
Tenderden, Kent Spinning
Wheel Restaurant & Antiques
Tunbridge Wells, Kent Halls
Bookshop *prints*
Reigate, Surrey Reigate Gallery
maps and prints
Uxbridge, Middx University
Prints *maps and prints*

Some other dealers in southern England

Bournemouth, Hants
Alister Mathews *drawings,
watercolours, old masters, by
appointment only*
Bridport, Dorset The Antique
Shop *maps*
Brighton, Sussex Bredon's
Bookshop *Sussex prints*
Nile House *Egyptian, Greek &
Roman antiquities*
**Broughton, nr Stockbridge,
Hants** V Mahy Ltd
oil paintings
Corsham, Wilts Farthings
Gallery *maps, prints, watercolours,
oils*
Denmead, Hants P J Radford
*old prints and maps, especially
Speed, probably finest selection in*

England

Dorchester, Dorset H V Day
maps, prints, watercolours

Eastbourne, Sussex E S Marks
Dutch masters

East Hoathley, Sussex
W A Sloane *Islamic art, Greek,
Roman antiquities*

Iden, nr Rye, Sussex Old Hall
Gallery *oils, (appt preferred)*

Lewes, Sussex De Montfort
Antiques *Islamic, Greek, Roman
art, antiquities*

Ryde, Isle of Wight Mitchell
Brothers

Salisbury, Wilts Salisbury
Galleries *marine, sporting,
landscape, military paintings,
watercolours, prints*

**Winterbourne Dauntsey,
Wilts** Winterbourne Antiques
oils, prints, maps

**Some other dealers in
Wales and the west**

Bath, Somerset H Parkin Smith
Dutch, Flemish

Broadway, Worcs Broadway
Art Gallery *Impressionist, Spanish*

Cheltenham, Glos Loreburn
Galleries *general oils*, Regent
Gallery *maps, prints, watercolours*

Chudleigh Knighton, Devon
Chapelry Antiques

Corsham, Wilts Farthings
Gallery *prints, maps, paintings*

Exmouth, Devon Warwick
Galleries *maps, prints*

Fairford, Glos W Pelly *oils,
watercolours*

Falmouth, Cornwall J Maggs
maps, prints

Gloucester J Walter *maps,
prints, drawings*

Hereford R Ward *Old masters,
nineteenth century*

**Kings Caple, nr Ross-on-Wye,
Hereford** The Hereford Gallery
oils

Penzance, Devon F A
Woolridge *oils, watercolours*

Shepton Mallett, Somerset
Grammar Galleries *Japanese
prints*

Shotton, Deeside, Flints
R Nicholson *maps, prints*

Stow-on-the-Wold, Glos
The Cotswold Galleries *oils,
watercolours*

Wem, Shropshire Grocott
Picture Gallery *English oils*

**Some other dealers in
midlands and the north**

Burley-in-Wharfdale, Yorks
Sylvia Head *oils*

Chester, Cheshire R Nicholson
maps, prints, Raymond Plant
sporting, military prints

Cuckney, Notts Dukeries
Antiques *county maps and prints*

Glasgow, Scotland E Alexander
nineteenth century continental,
I MacNicol *nineteenth century
English, Scottish paintings*

Halton, nr Lancaster, Lancs
St Wilfred's Antiques *oils,
watercolours*

Harrogate, Yorks Barnard
Galleries *sporting, flower prints, oils,
watercolours*, W F Greenwood *oil
paintings and prints*

Henley-in-Arden, Warks
Arden Gallery *oils,
watercolours*

Ilkeston, Derbyshire
R J Mitchell *Victorian paintings,
early oils*

Inverness, Scotland Northern Gallery *old masters*
Knaresborough, Yorks Thorpe *English and Continental oil, watercolours*
Leeds, Yorks Alexandra Galleries *oils and drawings*
Leicester Kathleen d'Offay *oils, watercolours by appt only*
Liverpool, Lancs Boydell Galleries *watercolours, oils, prints etc*
Manchester, Lancs Arden Gallery, Didsbury *oils, watercolours*
Nottingham Bonfiglioli *English paintings, drawings by appt only*
Sheffield, Yorks G W Ford *oils, watercolours*
Shotton, Flints R Nicholson *maps, prints*
Stratford-on-Avon, Warks

The Ruskin Gallery *English drawings, watercolours etc*
York Coulter Galleries *general paintings*

Some other dealers in East Anglia

Billericay, Essex B J Page *maps and prints – large stock*
Colchester, Essex Weiss *sixteenth to nineteenth centuries*
Framingham Pigot nr Norwich, Norfolk The Art Gallery *eighteenth, nineteenth century oils*
Norwich, Norfolk Mandell's Gallery *eighteenth, nineteenth century*, Paston House Gallery *oils, prints*
Swaffham, Norfolk Reiss Howard *silhouettes, miniatures*

Fine art at a reasonable price

In the centre of London is the *Folio Club*. Membership fee is reasonable and the club, which is just off Oxford street, is open for relaxation and refreshment from Monday to Saturday. The club provides the setting where *Folio Fine Art Ltd* offer original works of art and other collector's items at reasonable prices.

One tends to think of such things as illuminated manuscripts and Etruscan antiquities as being beyond the purse of the small collector. But this is not the case with *Folio* where the majority of items offered to members are priced between £2 and £100. The constantly changing display covers original etchings, engravings and lithographs, maps, sculpture and bronzes, drawings and watercolours.

Catalogues are issued at regular intervals for customers who are out of London – details of membership from Folio Fine Art, 6 Stratford Place, London W1.

Picture restorers and cleaners

London
B Brandt 69 Woodland Rise N10 883 0823
J Mitchell & Son 8 New Bond St W1, 493 7567
The Moorland Gallery 23 Cork St, Bond St, London W1, 734 6961
Pulitzer Gallery 5 Kensington High St, W8, 937 2647

Cheltenham
Loreburn Galleries 7 Montpelier Galleries, 56497

Edinburgh
Aitken Dott & Son 26 Castle St

Norwich
Mandell's Gallery Elm Hill, 26892

Liverpool
Boydell Galleries 15 Castle St, Liverpool 2, L Central 3256

Cosham
Farthings Gallery 7 High St, 2279

Leeds
Alexandra Galleries 30 Park Cross St, Leeds 1, 22719

Brighton
A Boyle Ltd 3 Brighton Pl, Market St, 26135

Chester
Catheralls of Chester Tudor House, Lower Bridge St, 20095

Stockbridge
V Mahy Broughton, nr Stockbridge, Hants

Some picture framers
A Hecht 326 Kings Rd, SW3, 352 1945
P Levi 37 Craven Rd, W2, 723 1948
A Ossowski 83 Pimlico Rd, SW1, 730 3256
H F Spiller Ltd 37 Beak St, W1, 437 4661
The Association of British Picture Restorers, 43 Ablemarle St, London W1, will advise on cleaning and restoration, write to the secretary

67

Chapter four

automata – clocks, barometers and musical boxes

The dictionary definition of automata is 'things which are self-moving or mechanical contrivances which imitate the motions of living beings'. In antique collecting terms, this means old clocks, watches, barometers, musical boxes, singing birds, and anything clockwork from an early Egyptian water clock to the first HMV phonograph.

The antique market in clocks is still surprisingly reasonable compared with other fields, but unless you have a strong do-it-yourself bent and are one of those people who can put the piece back again, do be chary of some of the bargains offered by general dealers with the vague remark that 'it only needs cleaning'. Unobtainable spare parts are costly to make, and if you want the clock to go it is better to pay more for a working clock or watch from a specialist dealer. Collecting fine clocks is an expensive hobby, especially if your taste is in French porcelain pieces, which I have seen in the most unusual shapes, such as an artist's palette, a violin or an old mill complete with moving water wheel driven by real water.

It is quite the fashion for women to wear a Victorian or Edwardian half-hunter watch on a long gold chain. This has given a boost to the trade in such watches which until recently have commanded a second-hand price equal only to their melting down value. These beautiful pieces, often set with coloured enamels, can be bought for between £5 and £10 and make impressive presents.

There is also a boom in barometers. Items which fetched around £15 a few years ago are now changing hands for three **69** times the price and, unfortunately for us, going to foreign dealers at a most depressing rate. An inlaid Sheraton stick barometer will certainly command a price from £60 upwards but the enchanting Admiral Fitzroy model, produced in Victorian times can cost as little as £5 and give just as much pleasure. Really early barometers, eighteenth century or older, are right out of reach of any but the serious collector and I have seen a reproduction Quare fetch more than £80.

Victorian clockwork novelties are a joy to collect, and even though Victoriana is fast on the way in, pieces can be bought for reasonable prices. Old stereoscopes through which one views sepia coloured three dimensional slides – rabbits which jump up and down at the turn of a knob and the multitudinous fairground novelties – are no longer to be found on junk stalls, but now command a real value.

Scientific instruments and animated pieces have a long history and can be traced to Islamic origins in the tenth century. Automata as we know it today really began to be developed only in the eighteenth century when moving figures and animated snuff boxes started to play sweet music or burst into chirruping song. The delicate singing bird box was first made in Switzerland when the intricate mechanism allowed a tiny bird to spring from its jewelled prison and give forth a melodious whistling sound. Such items of course, are extremely expensive now, nevertheless

Mr Porter of Hartley Wintney with just a few of his antique clocks. His family have been clockmakers for 300 years

more modern examples made between 1860 and 1930 can still be bought, but at prices about £50.

The musical box dates from Regency times and a collection is still within reach of the moderate purse. Most popular is the type which consists of a brass cylinder with projecting pins which produces sound when turned into contact with a resonant comb. Such boxes often play eight or ten tunes, the titles of which appear in illuminated lettering inside the lid. One can still purchase larger pieces too, which play on the insertion of a penny in the slot.

Books to read

Clocks and watches

Chats on old clocks *H A Lloyd* Benn

Clocks *S Fleet* Hamlyn 30s

Clocks and their value *D de Carle* Treff 30s

Clocks and watches *E Bruton* Hamlyn 25s

The collector's dictionary of clocks *H Lloyd* Country Life 210s

Country Life book of watches Country Life 42s

English clocks *M Goaman* Connoisseur 25s

French clocks *W Edey* S Vista 21s

The grandfather clock *E L Edwards* Sherratt 10s

In quest of clocks *K Ullyett* Hamlyn 25s

Investing in clocks and watches *P Cumhail* Barrie 50s

Book of old clocks and watches *Basserman-Jordan & Bertele* Allen and Unwin 126s

Old clocks *J Scherer* Hallwag 8s 6d

Old clocks *E Wenham* Spring 12s 6d (out of print)

Old clocks and watches and their makers *F J Britten* Spon 147s (out of print)

The plain man's guide to antique clocks *W Bentley* Joseph 16s

The story of watches *T P Camerer Cuss* MacGibbon 35s

Watches *Clutton & Daniels*
Batsford 147*s*

Barometers

**English barometers and their
makers 1680–1860** *N Goodison*
Cassell 168*s*
Old English barometers
G H & E F F Bell (in preparation)

Musical boxes and scientific instruments

Collecting musical boxes
Ord-Hume Allen and Unwin 42*s*
European musical

instruments *Harrison &
Rummer* S Vista 45*s*
**Musical boxes – a history and
appreciation** *Clark*
Allen and Unwin 42*s*
**Musical instruments in art
and history** *R Bragard and
F de Hen* Barrie 126*s*
**Scientific instruments in art
and history** *H Michel* Barrie
105*s*

An association of interest to collectors is The Musical Box Society, 11 Devonshire Place W1.

Specialist bookseller

Malcolm Gardner Bradbourne Farmhouse, Bradbourne Vale Rd, Sevenoaks, Kent, Bradbourne 51311, (new and out of print books displayed in a large room, in a private house). Please phone for an appointment, when you will be invited to browse around this large selection of bibliography on automata, music boxes, barometers, and all aspects of horology. Catalogues available.

Where to buy

London and the home counties

Charles Stewart Ltd of Wigmore St, London W1 probably have the largest barometer stock in England. They ship all over the world and are specialist restorers. Specialists in mechanical musical instruments, who will also repair, are rather hard to find. One such is *George Sunley* of The Music Box Gallery 81 George St, W1. He himself is featured, in fact, in our drawing at the start of this chapter. Singing birds and musical boxes are also the most important features of this stock. One of the country's largest leading restorer's of antique musical boxes is *Keith Harding Antiques* of 93 Hornsey Rd, N7. They also have a large stock of musical boxes for sale. *Camerer Cuss & Co* were established in 1788 during the reign of George III, and have an extensive collection of antique clocks and watches at their New Oxford St address. They also carry stock at 5 New Cavendish St. The fact that they have two large establishments is an indication of the important stock they carry. Expert repair work to all kinds of automata is also undertaken. Incidentally, if you have bought an early watch such as a Victorian hunter, it is much better to take it for repair to a specialist such as Camerer Cuss or in fact to any recognised dealer in such items. It isn't the fact that the workmanship is necessarily more reliable than the local watch-maker, but such dealers are more likely to have quantities of spare parts available from watches of the same period as yours which have been broken up, whereas it is unlikely that you have the same luck through a modern silversmith and watch dealer.

Stockists of one of the largest selections of clocks in the United Kingdom is the firm of *Huggins & Horsey Ltd* 26 Beauchamp Place SW3. They also have a range of barometers.

The name of *Aubrey Brocklehurst*, 124 Cromwell Rd SW7 is a must for the clock collector's address book. Close to the West London Air Terminal, a fine selection of mantle and grandfather clocks is offered.

Two more first-class dealers are *Charles Frodsham* 173 Brompton Rd SW3 and *D Boulstridge* 47 Lower Belgrave St SW1. Both are specialists in antique clocks and the former has been awarded the Royal Warrant, also *E Dent* of Pall Mall have a good stock and their name is celebrated for making the Great Westminster Clock striking on Big Ben of London.

In Kensington Church St W8 at the premises of *Philip & Bernard Dombey* are some of the loveliest clocks to be seen outside a museum. Specialising in French items, they also offer a fully illustrated brochure, showing a selection of clocks which include Meissen porcelain, Boulle, Ormulu and enamel.

The Regency House Marlow, Bucks are specialists in English and French clocks; and *J de Haan & Son* Waltham Cross, Herts have an important stock of barometers. Mr de Haan normally deals only with the trade, but will make an exception for the serious collector. First, however, please telephone Waltham Cross 22756.

At 93 Portobello Road I recommend *Graham Webb* who has a large stock of musical boxes, including the type you put a penny into and watch the huge brass disc move round whilst playing a gay tune. He also undertakes repair work.

Even if you're walking down Jermyn St with the sole intention of ordering a few new shirts, you won't be able to help stopping in front of *Graham Pontet's* premises at number 78. The display of scientific and nautical instruments, amongst a fine selection of early oak and period metalware is both arresting and beautifully laid out to catch the browsing eye. Mr Pontet has further premises in Mount St, W1.

Other specialist dealers known to us

Daniel Desbois Carey St, WC2 *clocks and barometers*
Prides of London Sloane St, SW1 *clocks and barometers*
M Ekstein W1 *scientific instruments and musical boxes*
K Harding N7 *musical boxes*
Philip & Bernard Dombey W8 *fine French clocks*
G Pontet W1 and SW1 *scientific and nautical instruments*
Stephen Lewis W11 *grandfather clocks*
Joanna Booth SW3 *musical instruments*
J Beare W1 *musical instruments*
E Hollander SW3 *clocks and barometers*
The Music Box Gallery W1 *George Sunley*
Wernik Antiques W11 *Ormulu clock sets*
D Young W2 *scientific instruments*
'The room at the back' W1 *clocks*
A E Gould SW3 *barometers*

Some other dealers in the home counties

Amersham, Bucks, Willow Tree Antiques *long case clocks*
Byfleet, Surrey The Manor House *clocks*
Dunstable, Beds W A Pinn *clocks*
Canterbury, Kent Five Centuries Art *clocks*
Henley-on-Thames, Oxon Market Place Antiques *scientific instruments*
Hertford Neale Antiques *musical boxes and polyphones*
Newbury, Berks Kennet Gallery *clocks*
Reading, Berks J Davis *clocks, watches, musical boxes*
Windsor, Berks Castle Studio *musical boxes*, R J Piner Ltd *clocks and barometers*
Woburn, Bucks C R Sykes *scientific and marine bygones*
Woodstock, Oxon Woodstock Galleries *clocks*

Southern England

Antiques through the post is the stock in trade of *Valentine Ackland* Frome Vauchurch, Maiden Newton, near Dorchester, Dorset. Miss Ackland has a clientele of regular personal customers and sends her goods all over the world. Musical boxes is one of her specialities and seriously interested collectors should write to her (with SAE) for further information of current stocks.

The name of *George Bell* instantly means barometers and he is the author of a really reliable reference book on the subject. Mr Bell has a shop in Winchester, next to the Cathedral. Here he sells antique clocks and barometers and undertakes repairs.

Peter Carmichael of Brighton offers a wide selection of barometers all in working order; and *Yellow Lantern Antiques* at nearby Hove keep French clocks in stock. *Paul Frank Ltd* have a good stock of clocks and barometers at The Green, Brasted, Kent. *Gem Antiques* Bournemouth, Hants is another happy-hunting-ground for timepieces.

Martin Hutton of Battle, Sussex is a must visit for the collector of nineteenth century English and French clocks.

Some other dealers in southern England

Bournemouth, Hants
The Studio *curio automata*
Bridport, Dorset The Antique Shop *long case clocks*
Brighton, Sussex A Alan *English and French clocks, especially carriage clocks*

Christchurch, Hants
G Hampton *clocks*
Hartley Wintney, Hants
Tessier *barometers*
Potbridge, nr Odiham, Hants
A Bird *clocks and barometers – an authoritative writer*

Wales and the west country

I don't know why it is, but dealers who sell musical boxes always seem to be particularly friendly people, perhaps it is something to do with a cheerful disposition which encourages them to be interested in such light-hearted things in the first place.

The owner of *The Treasure Chest* in Taunton, Somerset showed me some very fine specimens, including a musical train in glass case which ran over a bridge, in and out of beautifully worked tunnels – all to music, of course.

While driving through the West country once I took refuge from a cloudburst in what I thought was a bric-a-brac shop. My

rain-sodden spirits turned to delight on finding that I had unwittingly discovered a treasure chest of musical boxes and Victorian automata in the back room. I was offered not one, but a choice of fifteen HMV phonographs of early date.

John and Joy Rodber of Art and Antiques call themselves specialists in the unusual, and have a wide selection of fairground novelties – I was particularly taken with The Drunkard's Dream and some very fine examples of English and continental musical boxes which the Rodbers also collect. Musical instruments, from a harp to a harpsichord, are also stocked. This delightful shop is in Bridport, Dorset. If you're looking for a particular piece, telephone Bridport 2801 first.

Some other dealers in Wales and the west country

Cheltenham, Glos G Curtis *clocks*

Chipping Norton, Glos J Cleverly *long case clocks*

Chudleigh Knighton, Devon The Chapelry Antiques *marine instruments and scientific bygones*

Ffynnongroew, Flints

G Morris *barometers*

Hinstock, nr Newport, Shrops Smith *clocks*

Portishead, Som Curiosity Shop *long case clocks*

Stow-on-the-Wold, Glos Stow Antiques *clocks and automata*

Wells, Som E Nowell *barometers*

Midlands and the north

Malcolm Anderson of Plum Park Antiques, Paulerspury, nr Towcester, Northants, is a long-established dealer who always has barometers in stock. One model I saw was a coach-house barometer which had five dials, two of which were detachable. The thermometer dial would be placed on the mantle of an inn bedroom in Georgian times and the hygrometer dial in the bed itself. If either reading were unsatisfactory to the guest the management were obliged to put some more fuel on the fire or the chambermaid would be sent up to put a copper warming-pan in the bed.

Herbert Sutcliffe of Ing Hey Farm, Briercliffe, near Burnley, Lancs can offer a comprehensive stock of most kinds of automata, including more than 1,000 antique clocks, and he will ship

Wing Cdr and Mrs Guy Marsland of Littlebury, Essex. An excellent stock of barometers with a friendly welcome for the new collector

77

directly to all parts of the world. Just down the road, so to speak, is Brierfield and the premises of *J H Blakey & Sons* who are specialists in clocks and musical boxes.

On the main A41 from Birmingham to Liverpool is Whitchurch (Herefordshire) and *F W Hancock* who specialises in grandfather clocks. No early closing day there. *Patrick Kirk*, Knaresborough, Yorks, I think might be fairly described as a tuneful dealer, for his speciality is singing birds and musical boxes. Normally closed all day Thursday. *Barron of Stirling* offers fine barometers and also undertakes restoration.

A final note for those who have travelled in vain to find the piece of their choice – *Meyrick Neilson* of Tetbury in Gloucestershire claims to have the largest selection of English antique clocks in England. An appointment is advisable (Tetbury 201) and trains can be met at Kemble Junction station, by arrangement.

Some other dealers in the midlands and north

Pershore, Worcs Mercy Jeboult *clocks*

Leamington Spa, Worcs P Wale *long case clocks*

Leeds, Yorks L P Balmforth & Son *violins and cellos*, Olympic Galleries *string instruments*

Settle, Yorks Nanbooks *watches*

Sheffield, Yorks Ford *clocks and barometers*

Stainland, Yorks C Rycraft *clocks*

Stamford, Lincs T & S Hyde *hand made clocks in traditional English manner*

Stirling, Scotland Barron of Stirling *clocks and barometers*

East Anglia

I think the most energetic person I have ever met is *Wing Commander Guy Marsland*, a prominent dealer in barometers, weapons, naval and military items. He positively staggers other dealers by his ability not only to attend the early morning markets regularly but by the speed at which he covers the country on buying trips. The early bird catches the worm must be his motto. And this philosophy finds its rewards in an excellent stock of barometers which hang round the walls, and in rows on hangers like so many pairs of trousers! His interest doesn't stop at barometers and his shop, *The Old Carpenters Arms*, Littlebury, near Saffron Walden, Essex is filled with unusual types of marine automata, and military antiques of which he has a fine personal collection. He and his wife live on the premises and are happy to see serious buyers out of hours, by appointment (Saffron Walden 2546). The shop is closed all day Monday except by appointment.

For a business with a delightful name you can't beat *Riverside Chimes* Stratford St Mary, Essex, where you will find a good stock of long case and other antique clocks.

Some other dealers in East Anglia

Bungay, Suffolk D & H Llewellen *brass faced clocks*

Clare, Suffolk P Carrington

clocks

Stansted Mountfitchet, Essex M R Simpson *English barometers*

Restorers of automata

The Music Box Gallery 31 George St, W1, 935 4700

C Stewart 67 Wigmore St, W1, 935 3601 *clocks and barometers*

J Davis 14 Wokingham Rd, Reading, Berks, 63108

C Rycraft Scarr House, Beestonley Lane, Stainland, nr Halifax, Yorks, Elland 4255 *clocks*

Barron of Stirling 18 Baker St, Stirling, Scotland, 3693

R H Yeo Ltd 43 North St, Rochford, Essex

Garner & Marney 41 Southgate Rd, London N1, *barometers*

Heath, Hicks & Perken Hatton Garden, London EC1, *barometers*

The Belfry 121 Victoria St, London SW1, 944 9101 *clocks*

79

BLESS THIS HOUSE

GORDON HIGHLANDER

Chapter five

Victoriana

I have decided to include a section on Victoriana for two reasons: First, there are branches of Victorian art that have aesthetic values hitherto dismissed by the so-called purists of the antique collecting world. Secondly, because with the scarcity of pre-1830 items in the trade, and with more and more antique collectors coming into the market each year, young people can no longer afford to set their sights solely on the Georgian or Regency eras. The collector who happily forked out thirty bob for an eighteenth century glass rummer three years ago has to think twice before paying £5 for a similar piece now, and the hoarder of Georgian silver snuff boxes has probably given up hope of being able to add to his collection as he watches prices spiral. So, with the small-budget shopper in mind, some of the following notes on the Victorian and Edwardian period may spark off new interests for the collector.

Furniture

It won't be news to learn that Victorian furniture was usually ornate. Some describe it as ponderous and unwieldy for 1969-style living, but most pieces have a particular charm which I can only describe as cosy or homely – eliciting an immediate image of the Victorian drawing room – hub of a close-knit family society, where a large fire blazed within or below a rococo mantle.

Victorian craftsmen, on the whole, were plagiarists. They ruthlessly copied the styles of their famous predecessors such as Chippendale, but added their own squiggles, scrolls and

81

carvings at whim.

The Edwardians tended to take more delicate subjects as their models, so we see the finesse of Sheraton once more, coupled with the painted styles of Robert Adam. Although this is reproduction furniture or mock Chippendale, one cannot overlook the quality of the workmanship. The Victorian pieces were made to last, and what they may lack on finer points of design, they compensate for with durability. Some Edwardian artists were so skilled in their work, especially painted pieces, that only an expert examination of construction will reveal the copy.

The Victorian chair is the most sought-after furnishing item today. Probably made from rosewood or mahogany, dining chairs of this period are most elegant, although they now fetch more than £100 for sets of six. We all know the balloon-back chair, and the lovely velvet-covered button chairs which are so comfortable, and beginning to cost rather a lot of money.

Other typical items are, of course, the davenport – a ladies' writing desk with drawers down the sides and heavy carved-leg supports. Often they were inlaid, or had brass mounts. The chaise-longue – a hangover from the Regency period is worthy of attention, comfortable as well as attractive, and the military chest – sets of drawers with sunken brass handles for easy shipping and suiting the masculine taste. Originally supplied only through army contractors, they are now much sought after by dealers and the public alike. Papier-maché, is another distinctively Victorian design-style, normally small pieces such as round wine tables or occasional chairs in a dark background inlaid with mother-of-pearl.

Bric-a-brac

This is a term now used loosely to describe almost anything that should be referred to as junk, as well as those items which are bric-a-brac in the true sense of the word. The term really describes fine decorative pieces of the Victorian or Edwardian age which often had a functional purpose, and embraces a wide range of small objects of value other than jewellery. To quote Violet Wood on this subject, authoress and undisputed queen of the Victorian antique trade, '. . . bric-a-brac covers a range of small objects of value in an infinite variety of precious or semi-precious metals . . . most of the settings were of silver gilt, ormulu or gilt brass, and the objects so mounted could be made of jade, rock crystal, chalcedony, lapis lazuli, agate, cornelian – or set with river pearls and semi-precious stones.'

These days we can include in the term hat pin stands, card cases, posy holders, chatelaines and scent bottles. one delightful collector's item is the hardstone egg, usually made from alabaster or semi-precious stone such as agate or onyx and used by Victorian ladies to cool their hands before greeting guests.

Glass

This is an enormously interesting subject and I will not mention the plain translucent flint glass as known from the eighteenth century, since it is so much more fun to concentrate on the lovely coloured glass of the Victorian period. The various types of glass have fascinating names such as Mary Gregory, camphor glass, spatter glass, opaline, milk glass, satin glass, amberina and so on. There are too many types to describe here without making a total nonsense of the subject – so we recommend readers to the book list where they can cover the subject in depth. The entire category is described as art glass, which covers a wide field including America where items such as Tiffany and Burmese glass are prized collector's pieces.

Pottery and porcelain

Most of the major factories renowned for the delicate ware of the late eighteenth and early nineteenth century still continued to manufacture during the Victorian period. Differences in formula which had served to distinguish between factories at an earlier date were largely irrelevant by the 1830's when an almost standard bone china was used for making the basic items before decoration. A notable exception here is ironstone china – most famous of all being Mason's Ironstone. A tough formula, hard-wearing and with a clear ring when tapped hard.

While most of the dinner and tea services of this period were highly decorated, much of the decorative or ornamental items were exceedingly plain. Parian ware is an outstanding example and is mostly used for small statuary such as busts or classical figurines.

The most prolific of the Victorian factories were Coalport, Minton and Copeland, Minton being particularly renowned for the use of French artists and painters to decorate wares of the highest quality.

Gold, copper and silver lustre are all collectable items, and good stocks can usually be found in the north of England and Staffordshire. Jugs were the favourite design, but of course there are plenty of other examples to be found.

Decorated pot-lids and other items of *Pratt's ware* are much sought-after, and Rockingham animals such as poodles and sheep are worthy of attention. The latter, incidentally, make excellent gifts for children, being of interest to the children as well as of lasting value.

One of the most often seen examples of the Victorian potters art is the Staffordshire portrait figure. The Victorians had the rather gruesome habit of making pottery models commemorating some of the more colourful crimes of the century. Models would be made depicting the murderer, the victim and often the scene of the crime. Examples of these and other portrait figures are eloquently explained in detail in *Staffordshire portrait figures of the Victorian age*.

Victorian needlework

In some of its forms Victorian needlework is already described in the introduction to the *Carpet and textile* section of this book in volume one). Interesting items to collect are face screens, mounted or unmounted, used by Victorian women to keep the heat of the fire from reddening their skin. Beadwork bags – embroidered bell pulls etc. One word about lace: there's plenty of it around, and it seems a shame that after all the work that goes into making even the smallest lace-edging that there should be so little demand at the present time. So if you're looking for something to collect which costs practically nothing, try lace-edged traycloths which can be bought for about half-a-crown. If treated carefully they can be dyed to a more modern colour and laid under glass on top of dressing tables etc.

A real up-and-coming collectors' passion is Victorian and Edwardian greeting or Valentine cards. The most beautiful are made from embossed paper, which may be filigreed, sometimes on several layers, and then decorated with ribbon or lace as well as painting.

Cards of this kind can often be found in junk shops where a pile of old scrap books has gone unnoticed. The antique markets are a great source of supply here, and one or two shops mentioned in the London dealer section have a fantastic selection, coded and cross-referenced by almost every feature imaginable from betrothal cards to the eponymous fat-lady-on-beach ha ha ha ... type of card.

Miscellaneous collecting ideas for the Victorian and Edwardian period include *china boots and shoes*, from 10s to £5, a pair of course; *glass pickle jars*, from 5s to £3 for cut glass; *matchboxes and labels*, any price, known as phillumenism; *stuffed birds*, from 10s for a mangy seagull to £30 for perfect Chinese pheasants; *fans*; *scissors*; *ships in bottles*; *night-light holders* (they look like coloured paste pots) from 6d; *dolls* and *samplers* from £2 to £20.

Books to read

Art glass nouveau Grover (USA) 273s approx
Collectors pieces: jewellery 1837–1901 *M Fuller* Cassell 12s 6d
Coloured glass *Davis and Middlemas* Barrie 70s
Dolls *Antonia Fraser* Weidenfeld 30s
English Victorian jewellery *E Bradford* Spring 25s
High Victorian design *N Pevsner* Architectural press 12s 6d
Nineteenth century British glass *H Wakefield* Faber 50s
Papier maché *J Toller* Bell 35s
Patchwork *A Colby* Batsford 50s
Playing cards *R Tilley* Weidenfeld 30s
Pot lids *H G Clarke* (in preparation)
Shawls *J Irvin* Victoria and Albert Museum 12s 6d
Staffordshire portrait figures of the Victorian age

T Balston Faber 63s
Twentieth century paintings *H Jaffe* Weidenfeld 12s 6d
The Valentine and its origins *F Staff* Lutterworth 70s
Victorian antiques *T Shull* Tuttle 110s
Victorian china fairings *W Bristowe* Black 42s
Victorian corners *Roe* Allen and Unwin 48s
Victorian costume and accessories *A Buck* Barrie 50s
Victorian embroidery *B Morris* Barrie 50s
Victorian jewellery *M Flower* Cassell 10s
Victorian lace *P Wardle* Barrie 60s
A dictionary of Victorian landscape painters *S Paviere* Lewis 210s
Victorian painters *J Maas* Barrie 126s
Victorian painting *G Reynolds*

Victorian design register marks

Between the years 1842 and 1883 many makers of earthenware, porcelain and pottery (wood, metalwork and glass) protected their designs by registering them at The Patent Office. The purpose was to deter the widespread plagiarising of design work in this highly competitive period.

The basic device was a diamond with the four corners used to indicate the class of goods, year, day and month of manufacture, and the file number at the Patent Office where the registered mark was placed. Even today, information on any mark can be received from the Patent Office by application by mail to the

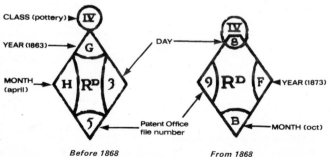

Before 1868   *From 1868*

Controller. You must enclose a postal order and a clearly drawn diagram of the mark.

As with silver marks, the year is indicated by an alphabetic letter, and so is the month. The date and file number appear in plain numerals, with the class of goods in Roman.

There was a change of style in the year 1868, the two diamonds with their variation are clearly shown in the diagrams.

Class of goods

I – *metalwork*; II – *wood*; III – *glass*; IV – *pottery*

Year letters

Alas, these do not follow alphabetically but have to be learned parrot fashion like a code!

Year	Letter	Year	Letter	Year	Letter
1842	X	1857	K	1870	C
1843	H	1858	B	1871	A
1844	C	1859	M	1872	I
1845	A	1860	Z	1873	F
1846	I	1861	R	1874	U
1847	F	1862	O	1875	S
1848	U	1863	G	1876	V
1849	S	1864	N	1877	P
1850	V	1865	W	1878	D
1851	P	1866	Q	1879	Y
1852	D	1867	T	1880	J
1853	Y	*new style*		1881	E
1854	J	1868	X	1882	L
1855	E	1869	H	1883	K
1856	L				

Month letters

Once again, no simple formula, just a learning slog!

January	C	May	E	September	D
February	G	June	M	October	B
March	W	July	I	November	K
April	H	August	R	December	A

Where to buy

London

It's a good place to start – London town. Certain parts of town seem to have almost turned into Victorian villages, judging by all the antique shops which have congregated together. Take Westbourne Grove for example, all along the Grove and into the side streets you can find Victorian boutiques offering anything from a transfer printed milk churn to sets of heavy moulded goblets, typical of the late Victorian period. Individual shops are too numerous to name fairly, but *Dodo* of Westbourne Grove is a special favourite, and a must if you're interested in household bygones. Similarly *Trad* in the Portobello Road offers everything from a ship's figurehead to a Victorian apothecary jar.

Another centre of Victoriana, which specialises in stripped pine furniture particularly, is the area just east of the Edgware Road before you hit the new Harrow road overpass. Take a good look at Antique City, 45 Crawford Place, W1 where *Joe Harding* has 10,000 feet of showroom on four floors. The services range from cloched fruit to stripped pine, and they often take orders from pop groups to decorate their new flats in bizarre colour schemes. The latest I heard was '. . . I want it all pine, but stripped and stained royal purple'. I'm sure the effect was magnificent, and Antique City will take care of it all from buying the original heavily painted piece to delivering the royal purple goods! Another enterprise under the same management is Junk City, 36 Bell St, NW1 in a nineteenth century milking barn with the original cobbled floor. The City is styled after an American antiques market and aims at being a wholesale warehouse where the trade can buy in bulk. Again operated by *Stephen Wood, Andrew James* and managed by *Joe Harding*, it is possible to arrange for retail customers as well as trade to make use of the stripping facilities available on the premises.

I have no idea where they get their own pine stripped, but there is plenty to be seen at *Big Deal*, 62 Princedale Rd, W11, and at *Things*, 72 Princedale Rd.

A great browserie of fine specimens is to be found in Kings Road, over the railway bridge towards Putney. Both *Avice Mostyn Antiques* and *Guinivere* at 578 Kings Rd specialise in stripped pine, although much of the stock is of earlier date.

Going over Putney Bridge and taking the first right, the Lower Richmond Road sports at least ten antique shops with a full range of Victorian items from fans to warming pans.

Having mentioned postcards, and Valentine cards in the introduction it would be criminal not to give the gold star to *David Drummond* ex-actor (remember Roger and Abigail on TV) who runs an exceptionally fine business in 11 Cecil Court, Charing Cross Rd, WC2 appropriately enough called *Pleasures of past times*. Mr Drummond is enchanting, enthusiastic and so full of *joie de vivre* it's difficult to keep up with his expostulations about his very exceptional stock. The prime interest is cards, Valentine, birthday, anniversary, fat ladies, hen-pecked husbands, views of Windsor Castle. You name it, he can probably produce it. Most of the stock is codified so well as to shame a filing computer! Also offered are prints, books on Victoriana, dolls houses and train models (836 1142)

Notable stockists of pottery crime scenes are *John Hall* and *David MacWilliams* at *Them & theirs* 17 Harrington Rd, SW7. They also stock postcards and are members of The Victorian Society.

If you're old enough you'll remember china fairings. Little pottery ornaments showing slices from life – usually with some moral or trite saying was inscribed on the base. They often feature as part of the penny-in-the-slot novelties at fairgrounds, seaside piers and even the children's section of the Science Museum! A dealer who specialises in these is *Bayley Galleries* Princes Arcade W1.

Who will light my way tonight? The question is answered – Victorian style – at *Christopher Wray's* lighting emporium at 604 Kings Rd SW6. Gas and oil lamps of the 1880s are the speciality, and they also supply glass shades in all colours of the rainbow. Lamps may be hanging, wall brackets, or free standing. The shop is a delight to visit. Pardon the pun!

No reference work on the subject of Victoriana would be complete without tribute to the fine selection of Victorian jewellery offered at *Cameo Corner*. Here, at 26 Museum St, Bloomsbury is one of England's best known antique jewellery shops which has recently celebrated its diamond jubilee. The business was created by a much-loved personality, the late *Mosheh Oved* who came from Russian Poland to England. Before he was old enough to take today's eleven plus, young Mosheh was apprenticed to a London watchmaker before he set up on his own in 1908. Alas, a mere ten days after opening, all his stock was stolen, and Mosheh was left penniless. Undaunted he took his remaining 25s, set up a new shop with borrowed stock, and never looked back. His first love was the delicately worked cameo – hence the name of the business, Cameo Corner, which has remained to this day, though the stock now embraces some of the most elegant pieces of antique jewellery, rare enough to tempt the late Queen Mary who was a regular customer.

Items are available at all price ranges, from a simple pair of cuff links to exquisitely hand worked collector's items from the middle east and China.

Before the days of movie houses and bingo halls, our Victorian great great grandparents amused themselves and their children with magic lantern shows, coloured glass slides projected onto a home-made screen in the drawing room. Often these slides would be of topographical interest, but the more delightful series told stories enough to make your heart bleed even in this rough and tough era. The slides were accompanied by spoken stories or rhymes such as my favourite, Billy's Rose, a sad, sad ballad by George Sims. To quote a little excerpt from this famous tear-jerker,

In that vile and filthy alley, long ago one winter's day
Dying quick of want and fever, hapless, patient Billy lay
While beside him sat his sister, in the garret's dismal gloom
Cheering with her gentle presence Billy's pathway to the tomb

She was eight this little maiden, and her life had all been spent
In the garret and the alley, where they starved to pay the rent
Where a drunken father's curses and a drunken mother's blows
Drove her forth into the gutter from the day's dawn to its close

Each verse would be accompanied by a different slide, and the place to find them now is the antique markets. They aren't at all expensive, but you may have to search quite some time to collect a whole set. I have seen many for sale in the *Blackheath Antique Market*, and of course, in the Portobello Rd, to say nothing of junk shops all over the country.

Coloured glass is becoming more and more popular these days, and there is a shop called *Victoriana* Church Rd, Wimbledon, SW19 which has a good selection. *Mrs Marjorie Parr* keeps some examples amongst her eighteenth century stock, in the Kings Rd as do *Peerage Antiques* 29 Thayer St, W1 who specialise in opaline glass.

There is a large showroom in Peckham Rye where *G Austin & Sons* offer an extremely wide range of furniture covering the Edwardian and Victorian period. These premises are well worth a visit since there must be at least three thousand pieces in stock at any one time.

The Camden Passage Antique Centre has a wide range of Victoriana for sale, especially at *The Corner Cupboard* 14 Pierrepont Arcade and *Greta Woolf* 12 Pierrepont Arcade who specialises in art nouveau.

Some other dealers in London

W2 G Hand *dolls*
NW1 Whytes *dolls*
NW8 The Rocking Horse *dolls*
SW1 Bayley's Galleries *fairings*
SW5 Kenway Antiques *general curios*

SW6 Bonnett *Staffordshire figures*
V Hall *general Victoriana*
SW10 Miss A D Hodson *needlework, bric-a-brac*
SW14 J & K Cameron Antiques *general Victoriana*

The home counties

Mrs Anna Browne has now extended her premises to include three shops in the High St, Harrow-on-the-Hill, 38, 40, and 46. She started in the antique business by taking over a sixteenth century houses from two old ladies and now finds that the personal touch which she believes to be so important to her business has enabled her to expand. A strong accent on Victoriana can be noted in her general stock.

Mrs Brown offers everything from button-backed sofas to Victorian perambulators and dolls. There is also a fair smattering of glass domes housing birds and fruit, to say nothing of apothecary's equipment and kitchen bygones of the period.

My goodness the name Deerstalker Antiques conjures up pictures! A new shop has been opened called this in Whitchurch, **91**

Bucks, on the premises of a 400-year-old pub called The Deer-stalker Arms. The house itself is at least a century older than the pub, so it lends itself pretty well to the antique trade, right down to the stuffed deer head (called Rudolf by the owners) which graces the inside hallway. Here we have true specialists in Victorian and Edwardian items. *Gina Wilmshurst* started the hard way in the Aylesbury covered market; her knowing eye for the bygone with potential has allowed her to set up this new antique enterprise with husband Roger who looks after the furniture side. The old beer cellar has been turned into a show-room for kitchen and country items (if you're athletic enough to crawl down there) while the other four showrooms offer a representative selection of stripped pine, door accessories, curtain poles, period costumes and coronation mugs. Take the road from Buckingham to Finmere and you'll go right past *Tingewick Antiques*. Only one shop at the moment, but another one opening over the road in a converted chapel during the year. A real browser's paradise of bygones and Edwardiana. The new shop will house Victorian and Edwardian furniture.

Willow Tree Antiques Amersham, Bucks have a really nice selection of Victorian jewellery, as have *Loco* in Paradise Rd and Brewers Lane, both at Richmond in Surrey.

The most marvellous bargains are to be found at Soulbury, Hertfordshire where *Sid Jones* has converted an old school house into an immense storeroom for bygones of the Edwardian and Victorian periods. You need a lot of patience to find what you are looking for, and I suggest that you know what you want before you begin the search. Hundreds of books for sale, and anything from an old Hoover to a shillelagh. One of Mr Jones best-selling lines is garden tables made from the iron base of treadle sewing machines!

Not surprisingly the name of the shop typifies its stock. An amusing browserie of Victorian and Edwardian items can be found at *The past era* Berkhamsted, Hertfordshire. Although they cannot always guarantee to have particular items in stock, there was a good range from stuffed birds to kitchen bygones at my last visit.

The cream of the Victorian period in terms of style and design is reflected in some of the stock of *Beckwith* in Hertford. They have a marvellous range of metalware, copper and brass especially, a lot of which dates from this period. They also offer choice glass and pottery amongst their general stock of early oak. The premises are currently at Old Cross, but after a recent fire which damaged one of the showrooms they may move.

The Bellows Guildford, Surrey have a good choice of metalware and Victoriana as do *G Lambert* Crescent Rd, Tunbridge Wells, Kent where you may be lucky enough to find pot lids and commemorative jugs as well as a selection of copper lustre pieces all mixed in together with lovely Edwardian and Victorian door knobs and fire irons.

Some other dealers in the home counties

Amersham, Bucks Willow Tree Antiques *furniture, jewellery, porcelain*
Blewbery, Berks Blewbery Antiques *general Victoriana*
Buntingford, Herts Peel House Antiques *general Victoriana*
Datchet, Bucks Silver Cottage Antiques *stripped pine*
East Horsley, Surrey Marjorie Quarrington *furniture*
Farnham, Surrey Venables *jewellery*
Richmond, Surrey Court Antiques *jewellery*, Loco *jewellery, bygones*
St Albans, Herts Dunnings Antiques
Wallington, Surrey Mrs N Knott *commemorative china*

Southern England

Trying to park is terrible in Maidstone the home of double yellow lines, but once you've found a spot a visit to *Mrs M Turk*, 4 Clarendon Place, will prove it was well worth the effort. All sorts of Victoriana are offered – glass, pottery, fire irons, flat irons, embroidery, curtain rods and picture postcards. Mrs

A thousand different kinds of bygone are always in stock at Dunnings of St Albans

Turk's selection of antique linen is quite something. She has a whole chest of drawers filled with the most delicate of lacework and embroidered tablecloths. Many people seem to think they are useless these days, but if you use modern dyes in the lovely colours now available, these fine pieces of work can be totally transformed. I have a table set of place mats and matching napkins in cyclamen for less than £3.

A nice selection of Victoriana and bric-a-brac can be found at *The Box Room Antiques* Alton, Hampshire. They have two addresses, Lenten St open in the mornings only, and Mount Pleasant in the afternoon.

Drusillas Antiques Berwick, near Alfriston, Sussex is run by *Pearl Boyd* at Drusillas Tea Gardens. Anything old, attractive and unusual is sold in this charming little shop – papier maché boxes, small furniture, collectors items mixed with inexpensive pieces for presents or to suit a passing whim. The antique fancier or dealer is made equally welcome. Drusillas itself has been established for fifty years, and is fascinating with its zoo, gardens, and thatched barn decked with old horse trappings. A new addition is a small collection of agricultural implements. Open seven days a week from April 1 to October 31 and every weekend during the winter, they serve coffees, farmhouse lunches and Sussex cream teas.

Another shop where you can search for goodies with a cup of coffee in hand is *The Hobby Horse* Alresford, Hampshire. All the cakes are home-made too. The shop is on the right at the top of the lovely square in this old town.

Just a few miles down the road is Winchester where *Mrs K M Shaw* has a good selection of Victorian porcelain, glass and other curiosities; you must also visit *Look* antiques, again in Winchester.

Some other dealers in southern England

Andover, Hants Antiques & other things *general Victoriana*
Brighton, Sussex Dragonwyk *Victorian pottery*
Bridport, Dorset J & Joy Rodber *general Victoriana and toys*
Bridport, Dorset The Hobby Horse *general Victoriana and toys*
Brighton, Sussex The Magpie

House *commemorative items*
Brighton, Sussex Harris & Son *general Victoriana, including a 10s room*
Canterbury, Kent Odds 'n Ends *bric-a-brac and general junk*
Havant, Hants Patch Antiques *general Victoriana*

Havant, Hants Parvo *general Victoriana*

Hove, Sussex Marian Craske *papier maché and Pontypool at fairs only*

Rustington, Sussex Mayes Antiques *Victorian and Edwardian*

upholstery

Hurstpierpoint, Sussex Lamb Antiques *general Victoriana*

Netheravon, nr Amesbury Wilts White Owl Collectors Cottage *general Victoriana*

East Anglia

It seems an anachronism to recommend *Sun Inn Antiques* of Saffron Walden as stockist of good Victoriana. Just listen to how *Nicholas Pevsner* describes the building '. . . a group of houses amongst the most precious of Saffron Walden . . . dating from the fourteenth century . . . with over-sailing gables . . . curved brackets, moulded bressumers and the most lively seventeenth century enrichments in plaster, geometrical patterns foliage, birds, and figures. On one house appears the date 1676 also the two figures of Thomas Hickathrift and the Wisbech giant.' Since Nicholas Pevsner is a leading member of The Victorian Society perhaps that makes it all sound a bit more in keeping. The shop has three showrooms, and is reputed to have been Oliver Cromwell's Civil War headquarters. There is a good selection of Victorian furniture, also fine glass and pottery, with a smattering of bric-a-brac and curiosities, amongst the general stock.

Right out in the middle of the countryside, a few miles from Newmarket, is Ousden and Cropleys Grove the home of *Mrs Violet Wood*. I doubt if there is any dealer in Britain with her experience of Victorian needlework, of which she has some truly superb examples in her home both for sale and for family living. She showed me some exquisite patchwork quilts and woolwork pictures. Mrs Wood's home boasts probably the only octagonal conservatory left in England, complete with stained glass. She also sells Victorian glass, porcelain, furniture and figurines and has expert knowledge of all branches of Victorian art. Mrs Wood is the authoress of *Victoriana: a collector's guide*, which I thoroughly commend to the newer collector.

Some other dealers in East Anglia

Attleborough, Norfolk The Victorian Cottage *dolls, needlework, general Victoriana*

Leiston, Suffolk Cross St

Antiques *fans*

Stansted Mountfitchet, Essex Simpson *furniture*

Swaffham, Norfolk Manor

95

Farm Antiques *Victoriana especially buttoned back chairs and sofas*

Swaffham, Norfolk Reiss Howard *papier maché, Parian ware*

The midlands and the north

An almost unbelievable collection of Victoriana, Edwardiana and what the owners describe as general junk is housed at 27 Watergate Row, Chester. Here *Erica and Hugo Harper* manage to keep four floors full with this and that – Staffordshire dogs, presents from Southend, implementa and impedimenta by the thousand and a huge selection of wooden-cased clocks.

Mr and Mrs Nat Gaunt of North St, Leeds specialise in curiosities of the Victorian period and one of their most popular lines is the conversion of brass lamps from gas to paraffin or even electricity if desired. Mrs Gaunt says that some of her best customers are the gypsies who love Royal Dux ware. She knows of one who has more than a thousand pound's worth of it in her caravan. There are four showrooms here, with some fine clocks and coloured glass, and a basement full of bric-a-brac, and shipping items.

Eureka Antiques in Northenden Rd just 4½ miles outside Manchester have three showrooms of shipping goods with the accent on Victoriana and Edwardiana and including a lot of stripped pine. The business is expanding so there may be a move; before making a long trip I suggest you telephone to make sure the address hasn't changed. (061-962 5629).

One doesn't know where to begin when describing *Mr Smith's* stock at Windsor House Antiques, opposite Leeds University. He has a large range of items, from oil lamps, Staffordshire figures, copper lustre and Britannia metal all beautifully arranged throughout the premises at 210 Woodhouse Lane. Mr Smith started his business by selling his own porcelain collection, and has never looked back. There is some fine Victorian coloured glass; whatever you collect you can be sure to find a item or two in stock however esoteric your taste – so no visit is ever a waste of time.

Some other dealers in the midlands and the north

Ashbourne, Derbys Ashbourne Antiques *general Victoriana*
Belper, Derbys Vanity Fayre *jewellery*
Birkenhead, Cheshire

W Courtenay & Son *Victorian art glass*
Birmingham, Warks P Greaves *jewellery*
Burton on Trent, Staffs

Some of the Pleasures of Past Times, London WC2

Cottage Curios, Coton-in-the-Elms *china, coloured glass*
Gt Budworth, Cheshire Ideas & Antiques *general Victoriana*
Ilkeston, Derbys R J Mitchell *Victorian oil paintings*
Leeds, Yorks J Hamilton Antiques *general Victoriana*, Smiths

Antiques *coloured glass*, Wallinet *general Victoriana*, Windsor House *fairings*, Witty *general Victoriana*, Woodruff *general Victoriana*
Liverpool, Lancs P Stone Antiques *general Victoriana*
Towcester, nr Northampton Sarah's Cottage *coloured glass*

Wales and the west

In the lovely village of Stogumber on the edge of the Quantock Hills, Somerset is *Billy Mullins* shop The Derby House. The main shop has choice pieces, mostly Georgian, but next door there is a converted stable shed where nothing costs more than 10s and the accent is on Edwardian bygones. Biscuit tins, tea caddies, ginger jars and meat dishes by the million. Good quality

Victorian furniture is offered by Philip Andrade at 50 Southside St, Plymouth, Devon. He specialises in interesting pieces costing less than £100 for collectors who want to furnish their home with tasteful antiques without going bankrupt at the same time! We highly recommend this shop, since it reflects the knowledge and experience which is displayed in the stock of fine furniture and furnishing items (mostly Georgian) offered for sale in Mr Andrade's premises at 3 Boringdon Villas, Plympton.

Some other dealers in Wales and the west country

Bath, Somerset Miss D Melhuish *Victoriana and curios*

Bradford-on-Avon, Warks The China Hen *samplers*

Conway, Caernarvon Black Lion Antiques *coloured glass, melalware*

Newport, Mon The Variety Box *bric-a-brac*

Rhos-on-Sea, Denbigh Shelagh Hyde *furniture, glass, porcelain*

Sherborne, Dorset Mrs G Young *bric-a-brac, Staffs pottery*

Tavistock, Devon Number Three Antiques *furniture and bygones*

Tetbury, Glos Nelson House *Victorian porcelain*

Worcester Doherty Bullock, Bygones *19th century art glass*

Choose to collect a few coins.

You'd be surprised just how many people go on buying 99 octane petrol for their car when all the time it could be running perfectly on 93 or 95.

But then at most petrol stations they don't get the opportunity to choose and do a little experimenting to try and save a bit of money.

Choose from the five octane grades in every BP Superblend pump. Buy the one that is *right* for your car. (Any BP station will give you the correct one if you ask.)

BP *sets the pace*

Index of antique shops

Antique shops are listed alphabectically by town. If you intend visiting, say, Harrogate turn to that town and you will find the twenty-one dealers I have called on or checked in the last twelve months. The telephone exchange, except where indicated, is the same as the name of the town or village. The number itself is the figure after the actual address. Be warned: these numbers are changing all the time as the country goes STD and automatic.

The only exception to alphabetical order is London. Because of its size I have grouped this separately at the back (see page 153). As there are more than a thousand dealers in London I have restricted those listed to those mentioned in text. And right at the end (pages 159–160) I have listed London's main picture dealers.

**ABBOTTS' BROMLEY
(Staffs)**
B Hammersley Antiques
Ivy House, 259

**ABBOTSBURY
(Dorset)**
The Salt Box Antiques
Fleet Cottage, 19 Market St, 232

**ABBOTS SALFORD
(Worcs)**
Brook Farm Antiques
Brook Farm, Harvington 244

ABERDEEN (Scotland)
John Bell of Aberdeen
56–58 Bridge St, 24828

William Young (Antiques) Ltd
1 Belmont St, 53757

ABERGELE (Denbigh)
Ideas
Bodoryn Bach, 2103

**ABERYSTWYTH
(Cardigan)**
W Trueman
15 Bridge St, 7642
White
3 and 5 Eastgate

ABINGDON (Berks)
Ingrid & Thora Lindberg Ltd
12 Ock St, 1495
R R Morris
29 Broad St, 776

ACCRINGTON (Lancs)
Graveson of Accrington
Sparth House, Clayton-le-Moors, 31746

ADDINGTON PARK (Surrey)
V M Baudoux
Fairways, Shirley Church Rd, 777 2339

ALBURY (Surrey)
H J A Huffener
The Street, Shere 2237

ALCESTER (Warks)
Harris Antiques
3 High St, 2200

ALDEBURGH (Suffolk)
The Corner Shop
2611
The Old Curiosity Shop

ALDERLEY EDGE (Cheshire)
Alderley Antiques
17 London Rd, 3468
Antiques
Brook Lane
The Gallery
Clifton St, 2522

ALDERMINSTER (Warks)
Paraphernalia Antiques

ALDERTON (Northants)
The Haven Antique Shop
Paulerspury 278

ALDINGTON (Kent)
S G Child Antiques
234

ALFORD (Lincs)
Denise Poole
South Thoresby, Swaby 259
Victoria House

ALFRETON (Derbys)
C B Sheppard
17 King St, 2602

ALFRISTON (Sussex)
The Urn
307

ALNWICK (Northumberland)
Post Boy Rooms
Louvre Restaurant, 2040

ALMONDSBURY (Glos)
The Manor House
Gaunts Earthcott, Winterbourne 2225

ALRESFORD (Hants)
Bay Tree House
26 West St, 2790
Bennett & Stow
25–27 Broad St, 2850
I H Doble
Beresford House, Pound Hill, 2869
Gore Langton
Pleasant House, West St, 2899
The Hobby Horse
6 Broad St, 2308
Itchen Antiques
16 West St, 2961
Look
22 West St, 2862
Number Forty
40 West St, 2453

ALTON (Hants)
The Box Room
13b Lenten St (am only)
4 Mount Pleasant (pm only)

ALTRINCHAM (Cheshire)
Q L Brown
24 Regent Rd and 6 Greenwood St, 5108
L H Gilliard
64 Manchester Rd, 061 928
M A Hawkin
11 Oxford Rd, 3846

ALVERSTOKE (Hants)
Alverstoke Antiques
47 Village Rd, Gosport 82204

ALVESCOT (Oxon)
Benjamin Porter
Shill House, Carterton 393

ALVINGTON (Glos)
Mrs S L Chislett
Bradstone House, Netherend 373

AMBLESIDE (Westmorland)
Brathay Galleries Ltd
1 Church St, 3291

AMERSHAM (Bucks)
The Antique Shop
10 Broadway, 1988
Collector's Treasures Ltd
91 High St, 2713
Forge Cottage Antiques
25 The Broadway, 3173
Hinton House
132 High St, 291
Vyse Millard
The Mill Stream, Old Amersham, 1023
The Sundial
19 Whielden St, 632
Willow Tree Antiques
Market Sq, Berkhamstead 6137 (priv; closed Thurs)

AMPTHILL (Beds)
David Litt Antiques
18 Dunstable St, 3067

ANDOVER (Hants)
Antiques & Other Things
11 London St, 2026 (priv)
The Little Gallery
90 High St, Weyhill 449

APPLEBY (Westmorland)
Au Bon Souvenir
2 High Wiend, 491

APPLETREEWICK (Yorks)
G H Sutcliffe
Appletree House, Burnsall 663
(appt only)

ARNSIDE (Westmorland)
Trevor Lee
Braeside, Promenade, 505

ARUNDEL (Sussex)
Christopher's of Arundel
30 High St, 3248
Friend Lissenden
49 Tarrant St, 3353
Arundel Antiques Market
Shipyard, River Rd, 2012
Sefton Antiques
71 High St, 2233
Westlands Antiques
25a High St, 3044

ASCOT (Berks)
The Old Clock House
High St, 22905
Piner & Woodley
Pheasant Cottage, Locks Ride,
Winkfield Row 2458
Somerset House Antiques
London Rd, 21968

ASHBOURNE (Derbys)
The Antique Shop
5 Church St, Kirk Langley 347 (priv)
Ashbourne Antiques
47 Church St, 2359 (normally closed
Tues, Wed, Fri)
Philip Horsley
30 Church St

ASHBY DE LA ZOUCH (Leics)
Huntingdon House
Market St, 2676
J & R Ratcliffe
102 Market St, 2703

ASHFORD (Kent)
Ashford Antiques
Market Buildings, Godington Rd, 22997

ASHTEAD (Surrey)
Cottage Antiques
Fowler's Cottage, Rectory Lane, 2123

ASHTON UNDER LYNE (Lancs)
Kenworthys Ltd
226 Stamford St, 3043

ATHERSTONE (Warwickshire)
Mercian Gallery
41 Long St, 2996

ATTLEBOROUGH (Norfolk)
The Victorian Cottage
High St, 3285

AXBRIDGE (Som)
Corner House Antiques
301

AYLSHAM (Norfolk)
Maltings Antiques
Millgate, 3137

BACUP (Lancs)
B J Davey & Son (Antiques) Ltd
The Clock, 127 Todmorden Rd, 966

BAKEWELL (Derbys)
K Chappell
King St, 2496
Maurice Goldstone & Son
Avenel Court, King St and The Old Town
Hall, 2487
Wyebridge Antiques
Bridge St, 2068

BALA (Merioneth)
Owain Glyndwr Antiques
Druid House, 219

BALCOMBE (Sussex)
Balcombe Galleries
415
The Barn Antiques
436

BANBURY (Oxon)
P Jackson
45 High St, 2099
Quantocks
3 Broughton Rd, 2162
Mrs E Smith
49 The Green, 2673

BANGOR (Caernarvon)
Leslie Davey Antiques
286 High St, 3053

BANWELL (Som)
John H Collings Ltd
Prospect House, Knightcott, 2148

103

BARMOUTH (Merioneth)
The Steps Antiques
33 High St, 643

BARNET (Herts)
Barnet Antiques and Fine Art Ltd
236 High St, Hadley Green 3620

BARNSTAPLE (Devon)
Blue Gallery
16 Joy St, 3536

BARROW (Lancs)
Barrow Antiques
3511

BARTON (Lancs)
W Parker
Garstang Rd, Broughton 2204

BARTON UNDER NEEDWOOD (Staffs)
Dieudonne Langston
The White House, 228

BASFORD (Staffs)
The Antique Shop
539 Etruria Rd, Basford, Newcastle-under-Lyme 69064
Tunnicliffe's Antiques
539 Etruria Rd, Stoke-on-Trent 69064

BASINGSTOKE (Hants)
A Dellafera
1 Sheppard Rd, Basingstoke-by-pass, 22286
George Phillips
5 Hackwood Rd, 23229
Philip Rogerson
81 Church St, 346

BASLOW (Derbys)
K Chappell
Goose Green, Bakewell 2960

BATH (Som)
Charles Angell
34 Milsom St, 22762
Anticus
19 Barton St, 3797
Peter Baxter
26 Broad St, 60781
Celda
11–12 Queen St, 22851
The Chatelaine
5 Prince's Bldgs, George St, 3747
Francis Christie
5 Abbey Green, 4476
Andrew Dando
4 Wood St, Queen Sq, 22702
Gerald Deacon
2 Wood St, Queen Sq, 25907
D & B Dickinson
22 New Bond St, 3502

Georgian Antiques
21 Broad St, 5850
Charles T Gilmer Ltd
16 Old Bond St, 3754
The Golden Era
10 Bartlett St, 60735
Valentine Gould
33 Belvedere, 5367
John Keil (Interior Furnishing) Ltd
7–9 Quiet St, 63176
Charles Lake
31 Broad St, 22873
E P Mallory & Son Ltd
1–4 Bridge St and 5 Old Bond St, 24147
H & R Marsh
29 Stall St
Miss O Melluish
13 York St
Morlais House
3 George St, 3211
T E Robinson
3a Bartlett St, 2782
M Sainsbury
35 Gay St, 24808
Philippa Savery
Abbey Green, 61855
H Parkin Smith
36 Gay St, 24305
F J Symes
12a Barton St and 1 Harrington Pl, 3772
Helen Watts Galleries
32 Barton St, 26020

BATTLE (Sussex)
Abbey Antiques
Old Church House, 3295
Mrs E M Byrne
Mount Joy, 31 Mount St, 2132
Martin Hutton
9 Mount St, 2715
Rona & Gordon Kett
Peppers, Mount St, 3144
E A Matthews
Old Guildhall, 2944
David Sutcliffe
Senlac House, 91 High St, 2768

BEACONSFIELD (Bucks)
Beaconsfield Gallery
27 London End, 2538
Harold Lee Brown
26 High St, 3045
Sidney Culley Antiques
Wycombe End, 3796
Richard Fairbairn
Great Oaks, Grove Rd, 4145 (appt advisable)
Hilda Gosselin
Harlequin House, 3948
Somerville Hough
The Yews, London End, 4022
David Messum
26 London End, 2242
Oliver Tribe
The Old Curiosity Shop, Old Town, 4473

BEAMINSTER (Dorset)
Anthony Jakins
7a Hogshill St, 479
Montague Rumsey
4 The Square, 417

BEAUMARIS (Anglesey)
Hermitage Antiques
Rosemary Lane, 471
Tudor Rose & Mona Antiqua
31 and 32 Castle St, 203

BECKINGTON (Som)
Monmouth House Antiques

BECKLEY (Sussex)
The Vines Antiques
300

BEDALE (Yorks)
Christopher of York Ltd
Carthorpe Manor, Sinderby 295

BEDFORD (Beds)
T M Read (Antiques)
3a Newnham St, 56568

BELBROUGHTON (Worcs)
F W Lambe
30 High St, 361

BELPER (Derbys)
Vanity Fayre
63-67 Bridge St, 2559

BEMBRIDGE (Isle of Wight)
The Casket
Sherborne St, 2734

BEOLEY (Worcs)
The Old Coach House
St Leonards Grange, Redditch 2145

BERKHAMSTED (Herts)
The Castle Gallery
87 and 115 High St, 4814 and 3106
J Hutton
108 High St, 5979
Christine Jeggo Antiques Ltd
135 High St, 4534
Leyton Antiques
114 High St
Northchurch Antiques Ltd
53 High St, 6355
F E Norwood Ltd
146 High St, 4361
Park St Antiques
350 High St, 4790
The Past Era
59-61 High St, 5742

BETWS-Y-COED (Caern)
Isaac Balkin
Cross Keys, 334

BEVERLEY (Yorks)
T Edwards & Son
Tudor House, North Bar Without

BEWDLEY (Worcs)
Stanley Fisher
25 High St, 3171

BEXHILL ON SEA (Sussex)
Stanley Courtenay Antiques
9 St Leonards Rd, 780
Forge House
Bexhill Old Town, 3188

BICESTER (Oxon)
D Lisseter
3 Kings End, 402

BIDDENDEN (Kent)
Biddenden Antiques
20 The Street, 339

BIDEFORD (Devon)
J Collins & Son
The Studio, 63 High St, 3103
S R Sluman
3 Queen St, 2696

BILLERICAY (Essex)
Brian J Page
Hill House, 24 High St, 53471
(closed Fri am)

BILLINGSHURST (Sussex)
T Thurlow-Smith
Antiques, 95 High St, 2554

BINGLEY (Yorks)
Antiques
84 Main St
Elizabeth Antiques
104 Main St, 3257

BIRCHINGTON (Kent)
Silvesters
2 Station Rd, 41521

BIRDLIP (Glos)
Antiques Gallery
Black Horse Ridge, Witcombe 2177

BIRKENHEAD (Cheshire)
William Courtenay & Son
Tunnel Entrance, Cross St-Chester St
Corner, 8693

BIRMINGHAM (Warks)
D & M Davis Ltd
3 Livery St, 236 1304
Ellis & Co (Birmingham) Ltd
Unity Works, Constitution Hill, Hockley,
Birmingham 19, 236-1742

Format Coin & Metal Co Ltd
269 Broad St, Birmingham 1
Midland 2057

Glencoe Antiques
82–84 Church Rd, Yardley, Birmingham
25, 021 706 3536

Perry Greaves Ltd
2–4 The Priory, Colmore Circus,
Birmingham 4, 236 9297 and
1–9 Corporation St, Birmingham 2,
Midland 5479

Harris Antiques
2071 Coventry Rd, Sheldon,
Birmingham 26, 021 743 2559

Kestrel House Antiques
72 Gravelly Hill North, Erdington,
Birmingham 23, 021 373 2375

Lisle Antiques
Camp Hill, Birmingham 12, 772 3683

Nathan & Co (Birmingham) Ltd
31 Corporation St, Birmingham 2,
Midland 5225

James Reeve
11–12 Cumberland St, Broad St,
643 0145

Thursday Antique Fayre
141 Bromsgrove St, Birmingham 5,
Midland 5360

Treasure Trove Antique Market
1852–4 Pershore Rd, Kings Norton,
Birmingham 30, 021 458 2219

BISHOPS LYDEARD (Som)
Hall's
Court House, Ash Priors, 402

BISHOPS STORTFORD (Herts)
M W Bush
7 Dane St, 3198

Windhill Antiquary
4 High St, 51587

BLACKBURN (Lancs)
The Antique Shop
33 Salford, 52629

The Galleries
27 Preston New Rd, 56185

BLACKPOOL (Lancs)
C W Allison & Sons
Pennsylvania House, 1 Barclay Ave, 63054

The Golden Age
7–9 Metropole Bldgs, 22869

BLANDFORD FORUM (Dorset)
The Candelabra Antiques
37 East St, 3652

The Gay Pavilion
4 The Plocks, 3259

The Paddock Antiques
7 East St, 2934

Peter Strowger Antiques
9 East St, 3567

BLETCHINGLEY (Surrey)
Alexander Antiques
1 The Cobbles, High St, 350

Oliver Mathews
The Old Tailors, 497

BLEWBURY (Berks)
Blewbury Antiques
London Rd, 366

Borlase
South St, 274

BODMIN (Cornwall)
Mrs H G James
3 Higher Bore St, 2622

BOELEY (Worcs)
Jasper Marsh
The Old Coach House, St Leonards
Grange, Redditch 2145

BOGNOR REGIS (Sussex)
G Bartlett
Charlwood St, 22014

The Findings
12 Steyne St, 4635

L J Hartley
7 Aldwick Rd, 3578

A Hewlett & Son
51 Aldwick Rd, 1408

A Kite
5 West St, 24166

Phyllis Marsh
Main Rd, Barnham, Eastergate 2075

Ursula Sichel
2 Goodwood Pl, West St, 21931

Turner Bros
Elmwood Ave, 22345

BOLTON (Lancs)
Prestons Ltd
2 Deansgate, 25476

BOROUGHBRIDGE (Yorks)
R S Wilson & Son
High St, 2417

BOSCOMBE (Hants)
Boscombe Gallery
14 Ashley Rd, Bournemouth 37219
Anthony Bridge
844 Christ Church Rd, Bournemouth
49040
K A Gray
841 Christchurch Rd
W H Harrison
1 Gloucester Rd, 36066
Norman Lee
790 Christchurch Rd, 34033
Mrs Margaret Reynolds
790a Christchurch Rd (*pm* only)

BOTLEY (Hants)
Botley Antiques
8 Winchester St, 2354

BOUGHTON (Kent)
O E & S L Hansen
119 The Street, 421

BOURNE (Lincs)
Tom Jones Antiques
The Mill, North Rd, 2278

BOURNEMOUTH (Hants)
J J Allen Ltd
1a The Quadrant, 20512
Antiquity
266a Charminster Rd, 52358
R Baldwin & Son
31 Southbourne Grove, West
Southbourne, 48343
L Beach Antiques
12 Post Office Rd, 23035
Eagle House Antiques
459 Christchurch Rd, 37111
Gems Antiques Ltd
Albert Rd, 27337
Lionel Geneen Ltd
210 Old Christchurch Rd, 22715
Betty Hayes
806 Christchurch Rd, Boscombe,
48778
Lansdowne Galleries
199 Old Christchurch Rd, 21752
King & Hayman Ltd
R V Stewart Ltd
202 Old Christchurch Rd, 21919
Howard Lington
126 Old Christchurch Rd, 21220
Rodney W Lytle
222 Old Christchurch Rd, 22504

Alister Mathews
58 West Over Cliff Dr, Westbourne
61547 (by appt)
Victor Needham Ltd
119 Old Christchurch Rd, 21515
Desmond Plowden
29 Poole Hill, 20158
R E Porter
2-4 Post Office Rd, 24289
S H & W P Reynolds
688 Christchurch Rd
Russell's (Antiques) Ltd
9 Richmond Hill, 25352
C F & T E F Sainsbury
361-363 Charminster Rd, 59271
P Stebbing Ltd
7 Post Office Rd, 22587
The Studio
Manchester Hotel, St Michael's Rd,
23333
R A Swift
176 Old Christchurch Rd, 21280
Westbourne 63045 (private)
Capt R J Tompkins
200 Old Christchurch Rd, 26693
Wessex Galleries Ltd
176 Old Christchurch Rd, 21280

BOURTON-ON-THE-WATER (Glos)
R Halford Bailey
Halford House, 601
Mill House Antiques
The Mill House, 656
Old Malt Barn Antiques
Sherbourne St, 156
Studio Antiques Ltd
352

BOWNESS ON WINDERMERE (Westmorland)
The Old Curio Shop
Church St

BRADFORD (Yorks)
Blenheim Antiques
283 Bradford Rd, Frizinghall, 47673
Quality Chase Antiques
51 Idle Rd, Undercliffe, Bradford 2,
38849
Strathmore Antiques
508 Halifax Rd, Bradford 6
T Thompson
332 Leeds Rd, 26054
J & W Tweed
408 & 410 Leeds Rd, Bradford 3,
23223

BRADFORD-ON-AVON (Wilts)
The Antique Shop
5 Church St, 3193

107

Avon Antiques
26-27 Market St, 2052
Beau Nash Antiques
13 Market St
The Bridge Antique Galleries
24 Bridge St, 2201
The China Hen
9 Woolley St, 3369
Michael Reeves
Moxham House, Woolley St, 2789
Eleanor Dudley Smith
The White House, Market St, 2417
John Teed
17 Silver St, 3370

BRAINTREE (Essex)
Eric Hudes
Park House, Bradwell, Coggeshall 342

BRAMERTON (Norfolk)
The Art Gallery
Bramerton Lane, Framingham, Pigot,
Framingham-Earle 345

BRAMPTON (Hunts)
A M Bailes
Hawthorn House, High St,
Huntingdon 3207 (by appt and trade only)

BRASTED (Kent)
David Barrington
The Antique Shop, Westerham 3237
Paul Frank Ltd
The Old Manor House, The Green,
Westerham 3236
Brian Kentish
High St, Westerham 3463
Les W le Serve
Southdown House, High St,
Westerham 3522
Mandey's
High St, 408
Old Hall Antiques
Betty Locke Ltd
Sundridge, Westerham 2589
John McMaster
High St, Westerham 3647
W W Warner (Antiques) Ltd
Old Forge, The Green, Westerham 3698

BRAY (Berks)
Chauntry House Antiques
Chauntry House, Maidenhead 25319

BRECON (Brecon)
E & D Odwyn-Jones
The Struet, 271

BRENCHLEY (Kent)
Brenchley Gallery
Brenchley nr Tonbridge, 2016

BRENTWOOD (Essex)
The Corner House Antique Shop
49 Hart St, 2622

BRIDGNORTH (Shrops)
The Curiosity Shop
Underhill St
H Foxhall
Underhill St
Simon Antiques Ltd
2 Whitburn St, 2097

BRIDPORT (Dorset)
Croft Antiques
80 East St, 2552
Philip Dawe
The Antique Shop, 50 South St
John & Joy Rodber
5 West Allington, 2801
also at **The Hobby Horse**
29 West Allington

BRIDGWATER (Som)
J Blake Camp Antiques
67-69 High St, 2578

BRIERCLIFFE (Lancs)
Herbert Sutcliffe & Sons Ltd
Ing Hey, Burnley 24225

BRIERFIELD (Lancs)
J H Blakey & Sons Ltd
5 Colne Rd, Nelson 63593

BRIGG (Lincs)
Cottage Antiques
23 Wrawby St, 3060

BRIGHTLINGSEA (Essex)
Morcombe's
London House, 90 High St, 2036

BRIGHTON AND HOVE (Sussex)
Abbey Antiques
134 Edward St, 0273 684981
Adrian Alan
51 Upper North St, 25277
Richard Alexander
Nile House, Nile St, 27344
Sidney Ansell Ltd
36 Castle St, 27973
Antiques
24 Church St, Brighton 1, 28341 and
18 and 59a Middle St
Armoury Antiques
47 Market St, The Lanes, 28022
Margaret Cadman
25 Ship St, 29627
Peter Carmichael
13-14 Ship St Gdns, Brighton 1, 23072
R S Chapman
19 Prince Albert St, 29974

Denys Cowell
60 Middle St, 26758
Marian Craske
29 Salisbury Rd, Hove 3, 773356
H A Davis
10 Duke St, Brighton 1, 25953
Mike Deasy
Middle St, 27663
Harry Diamond & Son
Martins Bank Chambers, Brighton 1,
29696 (by appt only)
Grace Doyle
9-10 Union St, 27596
Dragonwyk
42 St Georges Rd, 682083
Evershed & Sons
121 Church Rd, Hove, 2045
John Fileman
Ravenscroft
4 Powis Villas, Brighton 1, 25521
Four Leaf Galleries
19 Middle St, 29990
Gloucester Antiques
18 Market St, 682320
O J Goddard
45 Brunswick St East, Hove 2, 738632
Hare & Elyard
48 Market St, Hove 735205
Harris & Son
40-41 Castle St, 29947
David Hawkins Antiques
12, 15 Prince Albert St, The Lanes,
28106
Kingsbury Antiques
59 Ship St, 28058
Magpie House
27 Kemp St, 683892
Mrs V Newton Smith
46 Meeting House Lane, 24429
Michael Norman (Antiques) Ltd
8 Black Lion St, 28844
Quality Antiques
16-18 Meeting House Lane, 27852
Regency Antique Gallery
38 The Lanes and 4a Church Hill,
Patcham, 29435
Regent Antiques
12 Prince Albert St, 28840
Benjamin Sims
39 Upper North St, 28619
B J & G H Smith
39-40 Meeting House Lane, 25123
Sterrys
45 Old Shoreham Rd, 26807
Talbot Antiques
65 Waterloo St, Hove, Brighton 776647
Toby Jug Antiques
60 Middle St
The Treasure Chest
146 Church Rd, Hove, Brighton 31148
Trevor-Antiques of Brighton
14-15 Ship St, 26712
James Waring
59 Ship St, 28887

Elizabeth White & Partners
43-47 Upper North St, 28706
Yellow Lantern Antiques Ltd
34 and 65b Holland Rd, Hove, Brighton
71572

BRISTOL
Barnacre Antiques
Severn Rd, Hallen
Clifton Galleries
18 Clifton Rd, Bristol 8, 33415
David Cooper
75-76 Alma Rd, Clifton, Bristol 8,
34583
Derek Cornwell
14 The Mall, Clifton, Bristol 8, 39566
F G & M Cox Ltd
68a Park Row, 24837
Howard Thomas
Keswick Lodge, 52 Whiteladies Rd,
Bristol 8, 33428
Frost & Reed Ltd
10 Clare St, 52525
Goldfinger Antiques
12 Northview
Hall & Rohan Ltd
The Mall Antique Galleries, The Mall,
Clifton, 30358
E M Jenkins
52 Cotham Hill, Bristol 6, 33553
John Keil Ltd
51 Park St, 28016
W Maxwell
14 & 17 Christmas Steps
Peter Mitchell
82-84 Alma Rd, Clifton, Bristol 8,
38331 and 7 Lower Park Row,
20927
The Old Lantern
20 Cotham Hill, Bristol 6, 34397
Donald Puddy & Co
24 Upper Maudlin St, Bristol 2,
Winterbourne 3045
Quinney's Antiques
17 The Mall, Bristol 8
Regency Galleries
72 Park Row, 25652

BRIXHAM (Devon)
Frederick Braham
2 The Drive, Upton Manor, 3344 (by
appt only)
Courtney Beer
Milton House, 3195

BROADSTAIRS (Kent)
G Wimsett & Sons Ltd
5 Charlotte St, Thanet 61713

BROADWAY (Worcs)
Armagh Gallery
60 North St, 3371

Michael Brett
Picton House, 2475
Broadway Art Gallery
3237
Christie
Yew Tree House, 3169
Copper Kettle Antiques
High St, 3258
H W Keil Ltd
Tudor House, 2408
Marion Keil Ltd
Forge House, 3471
Gordon & Brenda Knight
88 High St, 3227
The Top Shop
High St, 2471

BROCKENHURST (Hants)
Stanley Blanchard
Greatham House, Brookley Rd, 2158
Willoughby Antiques
Brookley Rd, 3040

BROUGH (Westmorland)
Augill Castle Antiques Ltd
Augill Castle

BROUGHTON (Hants)
Victor Mahy Ltd
The Close, 331

BUCKINGHAM (Bucks)
The Antique Shop
62 Wells St, 3332

BUDLEIGH SALTERTON (Devon)
B & T Thorn & Son
2 High St, 2448

BUILTH WELLS (Brecon)
G & M Hughes
4 Broad St, 2261

BUNGAY (Suffolk)
D & H Lewellen
26, 28 & 30 Earsham St, 2875
Lambe & Munn
40 Earsham St, St Cross 243

BUNTINGFORD (Herts)
Peel House Antiques
95 High St, 431

BURFORD (Oxon)
R Bowerman
The Antiquary, High St, 2207
David Marsh
High St, 3226
Peter Matthey Antiques
The Crypt, High St, 2302
Roger Morland-Coon
The Great House, 2302

Sandford Shone
Grafton House, High St, 2222
Zene Walker Ltd
The Bull House, High St, 3284
Roger Warner
High St, 2114
Frank Williams
The Old Post Office, High St, 2128

BURLEY-IN-WHARFDALE (Yorks)
Sylvia Head
30 Main St, 2178

BURNHAM MARKET (Norfolk)
M & A Cringle
The Old Black Horse
Trimmers
(opp Post Office), 243
Cabin Antiques
North St, 441

BURNHAM-ON-CROUCH (Essex)
Quai Antiques
The Quay, 3351 (summer only)

BURNHAM-ON-SEA (Som)
Culverwell
23 Church St, Highbridge, 4436

BURSLEM (Staffs)
The Treasure House
138 Waterloo Rd, 88795

BURTON (Cheshire)
J C Rowse
The Chase, Puddington Lane, 401 (trade only)

BURTON-ON-TRENT (Staffs)
Arden House Antiques
Tutbury
The Old Farm House
Moira Rd, Overseal

BURWELL (Cambs)
E Barton & Son
Sefton House, 55-57 North St, 263

BURY ST EDMUNDS (Suffolk)
Dutton Brothers
89-91 Whiting St, 351
The Treasure Chest
55 St John's St, 3570
The Goff Galleries
4-5 Whiting St, 4165
F C Nunn
49 St John's St, 309
R N Usher
South Hill, 42 Southgate St, 4838

BUXTON (Derbys)

E Hockenhull
6 Cavendish Circus, 2046
Hockenhull & Needham
8 Cavendish Circus, 2115
Marlborough Antiques Ltd
1 Marlborough Mansions, 2640
Plant & Sons
6 Hall Bank, 3727

BYFLEET (Surrey)

Ronald Lee
The Manor House, 43346

CALNE (Wilts)

Calne Antiques
West Hill House, 3464

CAMBERLEY (Surrey)

The Antique Shop
94 London Rd, Hartley Whitney 2605
The Black Kettle
39a London Rd, 4750 and 21 High St,
23845
Clarke's Antiques (Camberley) Ltd
2 Osnaburgh Pde, London Rd, 22677
Neville Bros & Osborne
52 Park St, 4990
A Stokes
103 Osnaburgh Pde, 2605
Reginald Weare
The Mews, Woodlands Rd, 4546

CAMBRIDGE (Cambs)

P R Anderson
1 Jesus Terr, 59315
Malcolm Clark
33 Regent St, 57117
Collins & Clark
81 Regent St, 53801
Gabor Cossa
34 Trumpington St, 56049
G David
3-16 St Edwards Pass, Market Hill, 54619
Galloway & Porter Ltd
30 Sidney St, 51287
John Gardner
30 Trinity St, 52943
F E Goold (Antiques) Ltd
3 Pembroke St, 51002
Ernest Hilton
32 Trumpington St
Hilton Gallery
3 St Mary's Pass, 56886
I Laws
12 Lensfield Rd
H L Roe
31 Trinity St, 58007
Owen G Roe
1 Downing St, 54394
C P Stockbridge Ltd
7-8 King's Pde, 56677
W Stockbridge & Sons Ltd
25-26 Bridge St, 53500

Stanley Woolston
5a Pembroke St, 50108

CANNINGTON (Som)

A D Harding
The Lustre Jug, Combwich 342

CANTERBURY (Kent)

Broad St
Luigi Cox
26 Palace St, 62729
E F Cranfield
4a Best Lane, 5654
Dover St Antique Galleries
Dover St
Five Centuries Antiques
18 & 20a Palace St, 63379
Edna Gough
Tudor House, 8 Palace St, 66504
Odds 'n Ends
Thanet House, 92 Broad St and 47
Staplegate Antiques
24 Palace St, 63970
W H Stringer
The Old Palace Antique Galleries
45-46 Palace St, 64182
Sun Antiques Ltd
23 Sun St, 63854

CAPEL (Surrey)

The Treasure Chest
Main Rd, 2262

CAPEL ST MARY (Essex)

A Cooper
(Closed Sat am)

CARDIFF (Glamorgan)

Broadway Antiques
154 Broadway, Roath, 791261
K A Davies Antiques
248 Cowbridge Rd, 29989
Graham Lewis
171a Kings Rd, Canton
Owen's Antiques
1 Wharton St, 36369
Philp & Son
77 Kimberley Rd, 43826

CARDIGAN (Cardigan)

The Cardigan Book Centre
1 High St, 2704
Vernon Smith & Son
Bayvil House, 2654

CARLISLE (Cumberland)

James Clements
56 Castle St, Crown & Mitre Bldgs,
25565
Maurice Dodd
112 Warwick Rd, 22087
The Old School House Studios
Rickerby, 26527 (by appt)

CARMARTHEN
Collins of Carmarthen
7-8 Jackson's Lane, Llanstephan 315

CARSHALTON (Surrey)
Hanlon's Antiques
5 High St, Wallington 5664

CASTLE CARY (Som)
Roydon House Antiques
South St, 575

CASTLE COMBE (Wilts)
Combe Cottage Antiques
250
Unicorn Gallery
291

CASTLETON (Derbys)
John Kelsey
Swiss House, Castleton, nr Sheffield,
Hope 265

CASTLETON (Mon)
Albany House Antiques
Albany House, 509

CERNE ABBAS (Dorset)
G C Heighington
Long St, 238
Old Thatch Antiques
81 Duck St, 210

CHAGFORD (Devon)
Old Market House

CHAPEL-EN-LE FRITH (Derbys)
Gisbourne Antiques
25 Manchester Rd

CHARING (Kent)
Charing Furnishing Galleries
Sherbourne House, High St

CHAWTON (Hants)
Clinkers Antiques Ltd
Alton 2187
L Loewenthal
Chawton Lodge, Alton 3571

CHEDDAR (Som)
The Cheddar Galleries
The Cliffs, 584
Edward Hudson
Cyn-Coed, Silver St
Old Farmhouse Antiques
North St, 345

CHELTENHAM SPA (Glos)
Antiques & Things
11 Bath Rd and 22 Bath St, 24223
Bick
5 Montpellier Walk, 24738
W R Cambridge & Sons
145 Bath Rd, 54502
Cavendish House of Cheltenham
Antique Department, 100 The
Promenade, 21300
G Curtis
24 Suffolk Rd, 53828
Gladys Green
7 Montpellier Ave, 52088
John P Higgins
4 Oxford Bldgs and 1 Hewlett Rd,
High St, 23984
J Holmes & Co
1 Gt Northwood St, 52594
A H Isher & Son
19 Bennington St and Rose & Crown
Pass, 24822
H W Keil (Cheltenham) Ltd
129-131 Promenade, 22509
John Kesterton
Townsend St, 25882
Betty Kirkpatrick
The Curio Shop, 2 Royal Well Rd
Maret of Cheltenham
7 Montpellier Ave
Martin & Co Ltd
19 The Promenade, 22821
Patrick Oliver
4 Tivoli St, 53392
Mary Packham
7 Royal Well Pl, 53485
Pittville Antiques
2 Prestbury Rd, 52397
Regent Gallery
14 Regent St, 52826
Tony Reynolds
7 Suffolk Rd, 22374
Scott Cooper Ltd
52 The Promenade, 22580
R E Summerfield
1-2 Montpellier Ave and 21 Bayshill Rd,
56101
W & J Turner
22 Montpellier Walk, 22939
G A Ward
Loreburn Galleries, 7 Montpellier Terr,
56497

CHENIES (Bucks)
Norton Antiques
Chorley Wood 3173

CHEPSTOW (Mon)
Jeffrey Antiques
Bridge St

CHESTER (Cheshire)
Boodle & Dunthorne Ltd
3 Newgate Row, 26666
Cadbury's Antiques
Christleton Rd
Catheralls of Chester
Tudor House, Lower Bridge St,
20095

Collectors' Find Antiques
40 Watergate St
Erica & Hugo Harper
27-28 and 77 Watergate Row, 23004
G A Kenyon
The Olde Leche House, 21 Watergate
Row, 24742
The Lantern Antiques
11 City Walls, 26486
Lowe & Sons
11 Bridge St Row, 25850
J & S Newman
60 Watergate St, 20241
Richard Nicholson
25 Watergate St
Quinney's Ltd
49-61 Bridge St Row, 23632
Bernard Walsh Ltd
11 St Michael's Row, 26032
Watergate Antiques
36 Watergate Row, 645 2496
Wellesley Wilson
29 Watergate Row, 23836

CHESTERFIELD (Derbys)
J B Nadin
39 West Bars, Chatsworth Rd, 3352

CHICHESTER (Sussex)
R L Austen Ltd
75 North St, 82135
Iseult Beaumont-Thomas & Son
14 St John's St, 82168
Chichester Antiques Ltd
43 North St, 84882
Peter Hancock
40 West St, 86173
M A Hill
57 Pound Farm Rd, 83470
Little London Galleries
10 St Pancras, 84156
Nice Things Old & New
2 North House, North St and
3 Northgate, 84377/86455
**The Old Theatre Antique Market
and Art Gallery**
43 South St
Neville Payne (Antiques) Ltd
10 Eastgate Sq, 86696
Zene Walker
St Peter's House Antiques
North St, 82481
J F West
27 North St, 4469 and 3 Crane St

CHIDDINGSTONE (Kent)
Barbara Lane Antiques
Tudor Cottage, Penshurst 577

CHILCOMB (Hants)
H R Marden King
The Thatched Cottage, 3913

CHILHAM (Kent)
Chilham Antiques Ltd
The Square, 250

CHIPPENHAM (Wilts)
Violet Reeves Antiques
14 The Causeway, 2955

CHIPPING CAMPDEN (Glos)
Badger's Hall
High St, 406
Carrington-Bates Antiques
St Kenelms, Lower High St, 680

CHIPPING SODBURY (Glos)
Tudor Antiques
1 Horse St, 2186

CHIPPING NORTON (Oxon)
J Cleverly
7 Horse Fair, 2626
New St Antiques
14 New St, 2493

CHIPSTEAD (Surrey)
B L Merriday
10-12 Station Pde, Downland
55620

CHORLEYWOOD (Herts)
Tudor Antiques
Rickmansworth Rd, 3751

CHRISTCHURCH (Hants)
Gerald Hampton
12 Purewell, 4000
M & R Jenkinson
36 Bargates, 5840
The Treasure House
(nr the Priory)

CHUDLEIGH KNIGHTON (Devon)
The Chapelry Antiques
2123
R E Martin
67 Fore St, 2339

CIRENCESTER (Glos)
Walter Bull & Son (Cirencester) Ltd
10 Dyer St, 3875
Cirencester Antiques Ltd
Dyer Lodge, 17 Dyer St, 2955
Thomas Hudson
4 Dollar St, 2972
E C Legg & Son
29 Castle St, 512

113

Oxford House Antiques
London Rd, 2923
Syrena House
1 Cheltenham Rd, 2755
Thornborough Galleries
28 Gloucester St, 2055

CLACTON-ON-SEA (Essex)

Pennyfarthing Antiques
75a Pennyfarthing Old Rd
Ye Olde Tymes (Antiques)
27, 31 and 33 High St, 24801

CLARE (Suffolk)

P Carrington
Market Hill
Half Moon Antiques
High St, 507

CLECKHEATON (Yorks)

Joseph Clough
70 South Pde, 3874 (by appt)

CLEY-NEXT-THE-SEA (Norfolk)

Studio Antico (Daoh Marshall)
Berrington House, 513 (weekends
Easter to Nov only)

CLOPHILL (Beds)

Millhouse Antiques
The Old Mill, Silsoe 335

COBHAM (Surrey)

Arthur Lock
The Vine House, 2464
Miller's
Portsmouth Rd, 2415

COCKERMOUTH (Cumberland)

Rutherford's Antiques
16 Main St, 3065

COGGESHALL (Essex)

W & D Bull Ltd
Market Hill, 385
H & J Chadwick
14 West St, 765
Cumberland Row Antiques Ltd
Highfields, 331
The Guild House
Market End, 789
L E Howes
11 Bridge St
Mark Marchant Antiques
Market Sq

COLCHESTER (Essex)

Abbeygate Antiques
2-3 Stanwell St, Ipswich 56445 (out of hours)

S Bond & Son
14-15 North Hill, 72925
F R Cooper & Son
14 Culver St, 72968
Paul Dane
115 Crouch St, 3300
Thomas Dunford
The Georgian House, 8 Middleborough, North Hill, 78171
Partner & Puxon
5 & 7 North Hill, 73317
Elfreda Rowley Ltd
7 East Stockwell St, 73071

COLMWORTH (Beds)

Edith Compton
Chapel Farm, 312 (advisable to phone)

COLWYN BAY (Denbigh)

Antiques Etcetera
337-9 Abergele Rd, Old Colwyn, 55249

CONWAY (Caernarvon)

The Black Lion Antiques
11 Castle St, 2470

COOKHAM (Berks)

Cedar Lodge Antiques
High St, Bourne End 1433
The Dower House
Bourne End 23794
The Tarrystone
High St, Bourne End 20937

CORBRIDGE (Northumb)

Centurion Antiques
Watling St, 2377

CORFE CASTLE (Dorset)

Hatchard's
West St, 291
Hollands
The Square, 273

CORSHAM (Wilts)

Robin Eden
Pickwick Village, 3335
Farthings Gallery
7 High St, 2279
J Dudley Ost
Farthings Gallery 7 High St, 2279

CORWEN (Merioneth)

Owain Glyndwr Antiques
The Square, 217

COTON-IN-THE-ELMS (Derbys)

Cottage Curios
Church St, Swadlincote 6991

COWES (Isle of Wight)

Curiosity Shop
Bath Rd, 3851

CRANBROOK (Kent)
D Findings Antiques
High St, 2372

CRANLEIGH (Surrey)
David Mann & Sons Ltd
High St, 7
Toone & Partners
Caryll House, High St, 2609

CREWKERNE (Som)
B J Palmer
45 South St

CROMER (Norfolk)
Cromer Antique Gallery
Church St, 2355
Hill House
Northrepps, Overstrand 445 (appt advisable)

CROYDON (Surrey)
H V Fisher
8 & 9 Mint Walk, 688 6790
Sutcliffe's of Croydon Ltd
23 Brighton Rd, 688 1907
Trengrove
46 South End, 688 2155
J Yewdall
440 Kingsdown Pde, Brighton Rd,
660 9608

CUCKNEY (Notts)
Dukeries Antiques
Willow Cottage, Warsop 2354

CULWORTH (Oxon)
Danvers House Antiques
Sulgrave 307

CURRY RIVEL (Som)
Peel Barton Antiques
266

DARLINGSCOTT (Warks)
P Hare
Darlingscott Farm, Ilmington
372

DARLINGTON (Durham)
A Corlett
181 Grange Rd, 4794
R S Richardson
6–7 Post Wynd, 4860
Stella Rutherford Ltd
15 Grange Rd, 68934
St Leger Antiques
58 Coniscliffe Rd, 2109

DARSHAM (Suffolk)
F J Harris
Darsham Cottage, Hertford 4491

DARTMOUTH (Devon)
Agincourt House
Lower Ferry, 2472
J & R Cawthorne
7 Southtown, 2124
Cottage Curios
6 Smith St, Blackawton 338

DATCHET (Bucks)
Silver Cottage Antiques
The Green, Slough 45766

DAWLISH (Devon)
Arthur West
23 The Strand 3283

DEBACH (Suffolk)
Mrs Pirkis
The Collector's Room, Keens Farm,
Coakers Lane
(by appt only)

DEBENHAM (Suffolk)
Mrs A Ponsonby
The Old Guildhall, 228
Eekhout Antiques
33 High St
Flemings Antiques
High St, 422

DEDHAM (Essex)
The Antique Shop
High St, 3271

DENHAM (Essex)
Apple Tree Cottage
Mrs Last, 2219
(by appt only)

DENMEAD (Hants)
P J Radford
Furzeley Corner, Sheepwash Lane,
Waterlooville 3063

DERBY (Derbys)
M Bailey & Son
202 Burton Rd, 41157
Moore Bros & Co (Jewellers) Ltd
10–14 Curzon St, 44674
Miss A Morley
9 Uttoxeter Old Rd, 44391
Rudolph Otto
29 Queen St, 45288
F H Pratt
11 Friar Gate, 43003

DEREHAM (Norfolk)
Antiques & things to please
Moore Lodge, 79 Norwich Rd,
2630
The Curio
25 The Market Place, 2514

115

DEVIZES (Wilts)
Saville Antiques
37 Long St, 3559

DIDCOT (Berks)
W H Neal
114 The Broadway, 2119

DISS (Norfolk)
John Oliver
41 Mere St, 2662
J & E Kenchington
102 Victoria Rd, 2322

DONCASTER (Yorks)
The China Corner
22 Chequer Rd, 65909
T & A Lesden
23 Lawn Rd, 4874 (by appt)
Ye Olde Curiosity Shoppe
15 Bennetthorpe, 49592

DORCHESTER (Dorset)
Valentine Ackland
Frome Vauchurch, Maiden Newton 276
H V Day
New St, 904
G C Heighington
48 Westhigh St, 244
J Legg
Regency House, 964
Michael Legg
15 High East St, 1596 and The Old Malt
House, Bottom-O-Town

DORCHESTER-ON-THAMES (Oxon)
Joyce Chick
The Pigeons, Warborough 409
Elizabethan House Antiques
High St, Warborough 521
Eversley Galleries
Warborough 407
Halliday's (Antiques) Ltd
Warborough 301
Christopher Kemp
Bridge End, Warborough 595

DORKING (Surrey)
Eleanor Hutton
59 West St, 3777
James Jefferson
18c Horsham Rd, 3158
Scott Hudson Ltd
5 West St, 2335
Swan Antiques
64 West St, 81217
P W Turner & Sons
9–10 West St, 4243

DORRINGTON (Shrops)
Ivy House Antiques
371

DOVER (Kent)
Derek Hart Antiques
114–118 High St, 1080

DROITWICH SPA (Worcs)
H & B Wolf Antiques Ltd
128 Worcester Rd, 2320

DROXFORD (Hants)
Meon Valley Antiques
High St, 458

DUNDEE (Scotland)
Walter S Beaton
37 Albert Sq, 25388
James Hay
89½ Ann St, 24630

DULVERTON (Som)
Crispins Antiques
High St, 397

DUNSTABLE (Beds)
David Clegg Ltd
53 High St South, 63535
Jack Neal
136 High St North, Luton 4666 (priv)
Paraphernalia
163 High St South
W A Pinn
112–114 High St South, 62562
Alexander Podd & Son Ltd
57 and 63 High St South, 62842
Blaise Preston Ltd
152 High St North, 62595

DUNSTER (Som)
The White House
High St, 213

DUNTISBOURNE ABBOTTS (Glos)
The Cullings of the Cotswolds
Yew Tree Farm, Miserden 378

EARLS COLNE (Essex)
Charles Morse
The White House, High St,
Mrs Mollie Webster, 270

EASINGWOLD (Yorks)
Antiques
42 Long St
Chapman Medd & Sons
Market Place, 370
R B Kendall-Greene
56–58 Long St, 251

EASTBOURNE (Sussex)
Wm Bruford & Son Ltd
60–62 Terminus Rd, 25452
Compton Antiques
5 Grand Hotel Bldgs, Compton St, 27159

Fortunate Finds
10 Furness Close, 239 (by appt)
Goddard
1 Cornfield Terr, 30598
Ernest Pickering
44 South St, 483
Seldon's Ltd
40 Grove Rd, 5133
E Stacy-Marks Ltd
120–122 Terminus Rd, 20429
Winifred Williams
38 South St, 30780

EAST BUDLEIGH (Devon)
The Old Bakery
Budleigh Salterton 3289

EAST GRINSTEAD (Sussex)
Cyril Feebery
79 High St, 23745
Longley's Antiques
5 Middle Row, 25323

EAST HOATHLY (Sussex)
W A Sloane
The White House, Halland 243

EAST HORSLEY (Surrey)
Marjorie Quarrington Antiques
Old Rectory Cott, Ockham Road South, 3747

EDENBRIDGE (Kent)
Cheverton's of Edenbridge Ltd
Taylour House, 69 High St, 3196
The Millions
High St, 2548

EDINBURGH (Scotland)
Alexander Adamson
12 Randolph Pl, Caledonian 7310
V Alouf Brothers
39 Frederick St, Caledonian 5950
Paul Couts Ltd
108–110 Grassmarket, Caledonian 3238
and 101–107 West Bow
Harry Chernack
85–87 Rose St, Caledonian 3038
Crafts & Curios
7 Bruntsfield Pl, Fountainbridge 6021
E B Forrest
499 Lawn Market, The Royal Mile, MOR 3980
J Gordon & Gordon
10 Randolph Pl, Caledonian 1960
David Letham
74 Thistle St, 031 225 7399
Janet G Lumsden
51a George St, Caledonian 2911
George Neilson
12 Gt King St, Waverley 3417
Nicholson Antiques
3 Cranston St, 556 1842

Gordon Small
48a Frederick St, 031 225 7710
Jan Struther
13 Randolph Pl, Caledonian 7985
Whytoch & Reid
7 Charlotte Sq, Caledonian 1777

ELLASTONE (Staffs)
M D & P J Fradley
Ellastone Old House, 291

ELM (Cambs)
Peter Crofts
Briar Patch, High Rd, Wisbech 4614

EMSWORTH (Hants)
C M Murray
2 South St, The Square, 3257
(closed Mon)
Regency House Antiques
19 Queen St, 2257

ERDINGTON (Warks)
Kestrel House Antiques
72 Gravelly Hill North, 2375

ETON (Berks)
Eaton's of Eton Ltd
62 and 68 High St, Windsor 60337
Mrs Peggy Merrick
Quest (Antiques), 41 High St, Windsor 65058
John A Pearson Ltd
127–128 High St, Windsor 60850
The Rye Galleries
60–61a High St, Windsor 62837
Maurice Taffler Ltd
17 High St, Windsor 711
Thameside Antiques
64 High St, Windsor 61003
Charles Toller
51 High St, Windsor 62058

EVERSLEY (Hants)
S Montagu-Puckle
The Oaks Antiques, Cooper's Hill, Yately 3168

EVESHAM (Worcs)
The Antique Shop
3 Waterside, 2953

EXETER (Devon)
E Alnutt
47 North St, 59539
C M Brown
The Tudor House, West St, 75908
Wm Bruford & Son Ltd
1 Bedford St, 54901
Exebridge Galleries (G M Woodhead)
16 New Bridge St, 55957
Exeter's Caledonian Market
13 Lower North St

117

Half-Past-Nine Art Gallery
13 City Arcade, Fore St, 59896
Edward Kennedy (Antiques)
17 New Bridge St, 71416

EXMOUTH (Devon)
Mrs R Barton
14 Bicton St, 5674
Warwick Galleries
1a Albion St, 5995 (priv)

FAIRFORD (Glos)
Clifford House Antiques
Milton St, 367
Fairford Antiques
Market St, 385
The Orchard Antiques
The Orchard, 546
Wm Pelly
Milton St
Town Bridge Antiques
Milton St, 451

FAIROAK (Hants)
The Old Bakery Antiques
Botley Rd, Horton Heath, 1467

FALMOUTH (Cornwall)
Peter Jackson
19 High St, 313989
John Maggs
54 Church St, 313153

FAREHAM (Hants)
The Antique Shop
24 High St, 3727
The Elizabethans
58 High St, 4964
Roy Jeary
25 High St, 3727
Museum Tea Room
211 Castle St, Portchester, Cosham 78035

FARINGDON (Berks)
The Faringdon Galleries
79 London St, 2344

FARNHAM (Surrey)
Bourne Mill Antiques Ltd
Guildford Rd, 4925
G E Day
20 South St, 5043

B & R Elliott
61 West St, 5408
D & E Freeman Antiques
82 West St, 6837
Georgian Cottage
22 West St, 4747
Peter Gosling
24 West St, 6837
Wilfred Gosling
10 Castle St, 6342
P & B Jordan
90 West St, 6272
T & H Venables
Hamilton House, 92 West St, 5472

FARNHAM COMMON (Bucks)
Paul Rich (Fine Art)
Langtons, Templewood Lane, 4595
(by appt)
The Spinning Wheel
2 The Parade, 696

FARNINGHAM (Kent)
Peter Beasley
Forge Yard, High St, 2453

FAVERSHAM (Kent)
Arden's House Antiques
Abbey St, 2895

FELIXSTOWE (Suffolk)
P R Downing
166 Hamilton Rd, 4143

FELPHAM (Sussex)
Peter Hancock
45 Felpham Rd, Bognor 21056

FERNDOWN (Dorset)
Peter Dryden Ltd
Ringwood Rd, 3324

FFYNNONGROEW (Flints)
Gilbert Morris & Son
North Wales Antique Galleries,
Beechcroft Hall, Mostyn 241

FINCHINGFIELD (Essex)
Church Hill Antiques
Church Hill, Gt Bardfield 280

118

Hinckford Antiques
Shore Hall, Cornish Hall End,
Gt Stampford 225 (appt only)

FLEET (Hants)
Robert Alexander
11 Kings Rd, 3713
P Lambert
King's Pde, Kings Rd, 2198

FLIMWELL (Sussex)
Post Boy Antique Galleries
Hastings Rd, 666

FOLKESTONE (Kent)
Cheriton Furnishers
43 Cheriton High St, 75932
Nordens'
43 Sandgate High St, 38443
L Partridge
3 Sandgate, High St, 66477
Victorian House Galleries
149 Sandgate Rd, 53016

FORDHAM (Cambs)
Phoenix Antiques
6 Market St, 363

FORDINGBRIDGE (Hants)
Avon Lodge Antiques
Southampton Rd, 3275
Bridge House Antiques
2–3 Bridge St, 2555
S C Scamell
Avon House, 2277

FOREST ROW (Sussex)
Christopher North
Lewes Rd, 2746

FORMBY (Lancs)
Margaret Layfield
Ambrose Cottage, 113 Church Rd, 73058

FOUR MILE BRIDGE (Anglesey)
Den of Antiquity

FRAMLINGHAM (Suffolk)
Chapman-Purchas Antiques
The Mansion House, Market Hill, 747
Richard Goodbrey
328
Norman's of Framlingham
Church St, 500 (appt advisable)
Regency House Antiques & Art Craft
Church St, Market Hill, 553

FROME (Som)
Keyford Galleries
Keyford Elms, Locks Hill, 2681
Sutton & Sons
Vicarage St, 2062

FYFIELD (Essex)
Fyfield Antiques
Queen St, Waltham Cross 20342

GARGRAVE (Yorks)
Bernard Dickinson
88 High St and The Estate Yard,
West St, 285

GATESHEAD (Durham)
N Jewett
639–643 Durham Rd, Low Fell,
Low Fell 877636

GERRARD'S CROSS (Bucks)
Gwyneth Antiques
Station App, 84918

GILLINGHAM (Dorset)
Guy Turner
Harwood House, High St, 311

GILLINGHAM (Kent)
Peter Chambers
Tudor Barn, Lower Rainham Rd,
Medway 34581

GLASGOW (Scotland)
Ernest Alexander & Sons (Antiques) Ltd
22 Bath St, Douglas 0619
B Altman & Co Ltd
61 Dixon Ave, Pollok 3203
James Forrest & Co (Jewellers) Ltd
105 West Nile St, Douglas 0494
H Lyons & Son
61 West Regent St, Douglas 1833
Captain A McAdam
Bedlay Castle, Chryston by Glasgow
Tom McAuley
28 Nithside Rd, Pollok 0338
A Macdonald
188 Woodlands Rd, Douglas 4247
Ian MacNicol
48 West George St, Douglas 0039
Muirhead Moffat & Co
132–136 Blythswood St, Douglas 2115
S Winestone & Son Ltd
10 Sandyford Pl, Sauchiehall St,
Central 6924

GLASTONBURY (Som)
Primrose Peacock
54b Benedict St, 2089
(retail Sat only)
The Four Poster
2150
Monarch of Glastonbury
15 High St, 3220

GLOUCESTER
The Antique Shop
25 Commercial Rd

Mrs K Finch & Son
The Basement, 2 Wellington Pde, 26263
G C & I Frith
5 and 7 College St, 23105
K E Payne Antiques
Old Barnwood Rectory, 16 Barnwood
Rd, 25779
John Walter & Co
11 College St

GODALMING (Surrey)
John Hancock
19 Bridge St, 1302
Heath-Bullock
8 Meadrow, 2562
Stevens & Brown Ltd
Ardon House, Mill Lane, 3391

GODMANCHESTER (Huntingdon)
C J & B M Whaley
The Old House, Cambridge Rd,
Huntingdon 1269

GOMSHALL MILL (Surrey)
Vera Lloyd Antiques Ltd
Shere 2433

GORING-ON-THAMES (Oxon)
Bygones
Station Rd, 2677
The Goring Galleries
High St, 2759

GOSPORT (Hants)
Courtez Antiques
307 Forton Rd, 80702

GOUDHURST (Kent)
Jenny Brewsher Ltd
Fountain House, 223

GRANGE-OVER-SANDS (Lancs)
Brian Blakemore
Fernleigh, Fell Rd, 2290

GRANTHAM (Lincs)
Jim Baxter's Victorian Bazaar
33 Wharf Rd, 3977
Country Cottage Antiques
10 North Pde, 3348
Edward Cranford
34 Swinegate, 3561
Harold Nadin
109 London Rd, 562
William Redmile
10 Vine St, 4074

GRASMERE (Westmorland)
Telfords of Grasmere Ltd
How Toe, 263

GREAT BARDFIELD (Essex)
The Pomander
Vine St, 582

GREAT BUDWORTH (Cheshire)
Ideas and Antiques
The Barn, Brownslow House,
Comberbach 267

GREAT CHESTERFORD (Essex)
Jean Mortimer
Sugar House, School St, 261

GREAT DUNMOW (Essex)
Constance Chiswell
64 High St, 2388

GREAT HORMEAD (Herts)
Mrs Pines
Westons, 241

GREAT YARMOUTH (Norfolk)
Peter Howkins
39, 40 and 135 King St, 4639
David Ferrow
77 Howard St South, 3800
Malcolm Ferrow
6 Hall Quay and 1 George St, 55391

GRENDON (Northants)
Markham of Olney
Little Hall (by appt)

GRESFORD (Denbigh)
The Mews Antiques
Chester Rd, Rossett 516

GRIMSBY (Lincs)
P K & R H Leigh
Granby Mews, Bull Ring, 2597

GRINGLEY-ON-THE-HILL (Notts)
Chapel Antiques
Wiseton 320

GUILDFORD (Surrey)
The Bellows
78 Woodridge Rd, 5044
Christiaani
4 Tunsgate, 66442
J Dolphin
Woodbridge Rd, 5019
P H Gillingham
8 Chertsey St and Lyndhurst, London Rd,
5750 and 61952
Joyce's Antiques
13 Quarry St, 4025
G Oliver & Sons
St Catherine's House, Portsmouth Rd,5427

H B Purser & Son
St Nicholas Cabinet Works, Buryfields,
4090
Raymar Antiques
4 London Rd, 63090
Ye Olde Curiosity Shoppe
Friary St

HADLEIGH (Suffolk)
Randolph Antiques
99 High St, Woodbridge 2765
Isobel Rhodes
73 Angel St, Great Wenham 409
P M Skoulding
Barn End Antiques, 123 High St, 3164
Sun Court Antiques
High St, 3378
Taviton Galleries Ltd
Taviton House, 103 High St, 3300

HAILSHAM (Sussex)
Mrs Eileen Daniel
Thorpe House, Windmill Hill,
Herstmonceaux 2367

HAINAULT (Essex)
Shaw of London (Furniture) Ltd
Fowler Rd, 6105

HALE BARNS (Cheshire)
Cottage Antiques
Hasty Lane, Ringway, 061 980 7961

HALESOWEN (Worcs)
Windmill Antiques
95 Windmill Hill, Dudley 54815

HALESWORTH (Suffolk)
Georgian House Antiques
3763 (Sat and Mon or by appt)
A J Strange
154a Chediston St

HALIFAX (Yorks)
Antique & Modern Art
205 Kings Cross Rd, 66463
The Antique Shop
10 Rawson St, 54907

HALTON-ON-LUNE (Lancs)
St Winifred's Antiques
229 (Tues, Wed, Thurs or by appt)

HAM (Surrey)
John Manussis
Ham Common 546 0366

HANLEY (Staffs)
Five Towns Antique Shop
17 Broad St, Newcastle-under-Lyme
69064

HARLOW (Essex)
Rundells Antiques Ltd
London Rd, Latton, 22906

HARLSTON (Suffolk)
Harlston Antiques
11 London Rd

HARPENDEN (Herts)
Hammersley Galleries
Pevensey, 12 Roundwood Lane, 4053
(by appt only)

HARROGATE (Yorks)
Robert Aagard
2 Montpellier Gdns, 5201
The Attic
7 Station Pde, 68669
Barnard Galleries
1 Crown Pl, 3190
A M Beevers
1 Montpellier Gdns, 4285
W F Greenwood & Sons Ltd
2–3 Crown Pl, 4467
Mrs E M Hardy
16 Montpellier Pde, 4493
Charles Lumb & Sons Ltd
34 Montpellier Pde, 3776
Minstrel Antiques
Regent Pde, 66653
James Ogden & Sons Ltd
38 James St, 4123
Omar (Harrogate) Ltd
8–10 Crescent Rd, 3675
Oriental Art Ware
12 Crescent Rd
J M & E Rawson-Lax
3 Cheltenham Pde
Frank Sanderson
3 Montpellier Gdns, 2687
F B Shaftoe
17–18 Regent Pde, 2151
Shaw Brothers
21 Montpellier Pde
Sidwell Antiques
20 Regent Pde, 66339
Smith's The Rink Ltd
Dragon Rd, 3217
Walter Waddingham
10 Royal Pde, 5797
Christopher Warner
15 Princes St, 3617
Miss N Wilson
19 Cold Bath Rd, 68718
A Year Dot Shop
14 Kings Rd, Ripley 540

HARROW-ON-THE-HILL (Middlesex)
Anna Browne
38, 40 and 46 High St, 422 4820

HARTLEY WINTNEY (Hants)
M Crawford-Holden
2152
M B McMillan (Antiques)
Old Forge Cottage, The Green, 2287
Porter Antiques
High St, 2676
W & E Tessier Ltd
Crown House, 2318

HASLEMERE (Surrey)
David Clark
11a Kings Rd, Liphook 3277
R R Glover
Antiques, Grayswood, 2184
T Glover
Town House, High St, 3868

HASLINGDEN (Lancs)
R & N Almond
176–180 Blackburn Rd, Rossendale 3413
R and L Greenwood
Clifton House, Blackburn Rd, 4895

HASTINGS (Sussex)
R A Brimmell
St Clements House, 29 Croft Rd, 409
(booksellers only)
Rye Antiques
91 High Street, 29758

HATFIELD (Herts)
Grejoron Antiques
Birchwood Farm Cott, 1 Northfield,
Birchwood Estate, 62537
Hatters Castle Antiques
44 Fore St, Old Hatfield, 64183

HATFIELD BROAD OAK (Essex)
Broad Oak Antiques
279

HAVANT (Hants)
Cargoes Antiques
2 Prince George St
Parvo
Penny House, 10 North St, 4813
Patch Antiques
8 North St, 3638
Vine Antiques
Chippendale House, Prince George St,
3435

HAVERFORDWEST (Pembroke)
Gerald Oliver Antiques
14 Albany Terr, St Thomas Green, 2794
and Johnston 483

HAVERHILL (Suffolk)
Barton Place Antiques
Kedington, 2035/2916

HAWKHURST (Kent)
The Antique Shop
Smugglers Den, 3356
H & C M T Cotton
Ellerslie House, 2161 (by appt)
Dymoke House Antiques
Highgate, 3265
The Hawkhurst Antique Galleries
Highgate, 2150
G Burman Lowe
St Margarets Cross, 3355

HAWKLEY (Hants)
Hawkley Antiques
The Old Bakery, Upper Green, 316

HAY-ON-WYE (Hereford)
Clive Grant
39 Lion St, 533

HAYLE (Cornwall)
A W Glasby & Son
Leedstown, Leedstown 303

HAYLING ISLAND (Hants)
R Lawson
82 Station Rd, 3623

HEACHAM (Norfolk)
George Robinson & Son
Pear Tree House, 228

HEADCORN (Kent)
Robin Bellamy Antiques
The High St, 401

HELSTON (Cornwall)
Michael Verity
10 Wendron St, 2423

HEMEL HEMPSTEAD (Herts)
Marchmont Antiques
56 High St (Old Town), 55324 (priv)
Look In
17 High St, 4329

HENLEY-IN-ARDEN (Warks)
Arden Gallery
High St, 2520
R Ferneyhough
Brook House, 2451
Jasper Marsh
3 High St
Zwan Antiques
69 High St, 2069

HENLEY-ON-THAMES (Oxon)
Adam House Ltd
71 Bell St, 3679
Friday St Antiques
16 Friday St, 2280
Henley Antiques
59 Reading Rd, 2848

Hill-Mayo Antiques
Old Armistice House, 33 Hart St, 3102
Market Place Antiques
35 Market Pl, 2387
B R Ryland
75 Reading Rd, 3663

HEREFORD
A Clarke & Son
84–86 Widemarsh St, 67426
J W Stephen & Sons
26–27 Church St, 4340
Russell Ward & Sons
37 Church St, 4036

HERSHAM (Surrey)
Douglas Franks
Lytheys, At the roundabout, 40145

HERTFORD
Beckwith & Son
Old Cross, 433 2079
F J Harris Ltd
11 Old Cross, 4491
Neale Antiques
21 Old Cross, 5347
L Partridge
25 St Andrews St, 4385
Michael Rochford
8 St Andrew St, 5291

HESWALL (Cheshire)
C Rosenberg
120–122 Telegraph Rd, 1053 (Fri–Sat only)

HEXHAM (Northumberland)
Arthur Boaden
27–30 Market Pl and 11 Market St, 3187
Roger Freer
50 Fore St, 2249
J A & T Hedley
3 St Mary's Chare, 2317
Mary Laws
Oak Lea, 3184 (by appt only)

HIGHCLERE (Berks)
Griffons Court
247

HIGH WYCOMBE (Bucks)
Beechdean Bygones
The Old House, North Dean, Hughenden, Naphill 2143
E M F Brown (Quality Town) Ltd
Church Lane, High St, West Wycombe, 24537
Sladmore Antique Gallery
Cryers Hill, Holmer Green 2279
Tythe Barn Antiques
Bassetbury Lane, London Rd, 22507

HINCKLEY (Leics)
Castle Galleries
114 Castle St, 3215 (closed Thurs)

HINDHEAD (Surrey)
Kay Catlin
7–8 Crossways Rd, Grayshott, 1608
Hindhead Galleries
137 (closed Mon)
C S Moreton (Antiques)
Bramshott Chase, 488

HINDON (Wilts)
The Old Bakery
235

HINSTOCK (Shrops)
R G Smith & Son

HITCHIN (Herts)
Phillips of Hitchin (Antiques) Ltd
The Manor House, 2067
Roslyn House Galleries Ltd
7–8 Sun St, 4774

HODDESDON (Herts)
The House of Whiting
66 High St, 3483

HOLLINGBOURNE (Kent)
The Old Forge
Pilgrims Way, 360

HOLT (Norfolk)
Anna Adams Antiques
The Antique Shop, Norwich Rd, 3167
Eileen Ringer Antiques
30 High St, 296

HONITON (Devon)
John Bryant
8 High St, 2446
G Noel Butler
Marwood House, 2934
L J Huggett & Son
Bramble Cross, Exeter Rd, 2043
The Old Curiosity Shop
71 High St, 2640
R G Rummery Ltd
Ernsborough Lodge, Exeter Rd, 2266
Geoffrey H Woodhead
Monkton House, 53 High St, 2969

HOPE (Derbys)
Antique Shop
Edale Rd

HORNCASTLE (Lincs)
H Baker & Son
14 East St, 3326
Milestone Antiques
48 North St, 2238

HORSFORTH (Yorks)
Lisa Taylor Antique Shop
60 Featherbank Lane, Rawdon 3617

123

HORSHAM (Sussex)

Causeway Antiques
11 Market Sq, 3320
Farthing Hill House Antiques
Broadbridge Heath, 2895
Pragnell & Co Ltd
42 Brighton Rd, 3470
Swan Antiques
Swan Yard, West St, 60033

HUCCLECOTE (Glos)

Stable Antiques
5 Glenville Parade, Gloucester 66977

HUDDERSFIELD (Yorks)

Mrs Ethel Woods
21 Beast Market, 25189

HULL (Yorks)

Antiques
Burton Constable, nr Hull,
Skirlaugh 400
L Rapstone
11 Savile St, Central 29640

HUNGERFORD (Berks)

Mary Bellis
Charnham Cl, 2620
Aubrey C Burton
The Pound Cottage, Charnham St, 2897
M Jarvis (Antiques) Ltd
Faulknor Sq, Bath Rd, 2203
The Old Malthouse
15 Bridge St, 2209
Riverside Antiques
Riverside, 2314
Wilkinson's Cottage Antiques
27-28 Charnham St, 404

HUNSTON (Sussex)

Frensham House
Selsey House, Chichester 82660

HURLEY (Berks)

Michael Thomas
Hurley Manor, 221

HURST GREEN (Sussex)

The Chessboard
127 London Rd, 252
H Simpson
Little Bernhurst, 345

HURSTPIERPOINT (Sussex)

Lamb Antiques
Cuckfield Rd, 2697

HYTHE (Kent)

E A Bennett
125 High St, 66071

ICKLESHAM (Sussex)

Vercasson (1966) Ltd
Old Oast Pl, 232

ILCHESTER (Som)

Sydney Vaux & Sons
The Antique Galleries, 228

ILFORD (Essex)

Harry Hollenberg
10 Evanston Gdns, 554 4860

ILKESTON (Derbys)

R J Mitchell
2-3 Station Rd, 2782

ILKLEY (Yorks)

The Century Antiques Ltd
35 The Grove, 4292
S M Collins Antiques
105 Leeds Rd, 4272
J H Cooper & Son (Ilkley) Ltd
31-35 Church St, 2595

ILMINSTER (Som)

Moolham Mill Antiques
Moolham Lane, 2480

INVERNESS (Scotland)

J F Kelly
32a Church St, 31777
The Northern Gallery
1 New Market Entry, Church St, 30278

IPSWICH (Suffolk)

April Antiques
St Stephens Lane
Atfield & Beckwith
17 St Stephens Lane, 51158
D T Cook Antiques
Orwell Lodge, 480 Wherstead Rd, 54320
(by appt only to retail trade)

124

David Gibbins
46 Burlington Rd, Handford Rd, 53708
Green & Hatfield
Northgate St, 53418
R J Hubbard
5 Fonnerean Rd, 54918
R W Paul
20a and 22 Fore St, 51696
Patrick Taylor
35 Elm Hill, 58578

ISLEWORTH (Middx)
Crowther of Syon Lodge
Syon Lodge, Busch Corner, 560 7978
Isleworth Antiques
The Old Blue School, Lower Sq,
Old Isleworth, 0342

IVYBRIDGE (Devon)
Mr & Mrs Gregory
Ermefield House, Western Rd, 304

IXWORTH (Suffolk)
E W Cousins & Son
Pakenham 254

KEDINGTON (Suffolk)
Barton Place Antiques
Haverhill 2035

KEGWORTH (Leics)
Christine McKay
The Great House, London Rd
(trade only)

KEIGHLEY (Yorks)
R T Clough
Stoneleigh House, Utley, 5222 (by appt)
Dunkirk Cottage Antiques
The Barn, Sandbeds, Bradford Rd, 5819

KELVEDON (Essex)
Kelvedon Antiques (James Billings)
High St, 557
G T Ratcliffe Ltd
Durwards Hall, 234/5/6 (trade only)

KENDAL (Westmorland)
Bell and Edmondson
147 Highgate, 2279
Richard Phillips
The Malt Kiln, 1225
William Sprinks Ltd
106 Highgate, 745
E Waller
146 Highgate, 1098

KENILWORTH (Warks)
Patrick P Morley
The Castle Green Gallery, Castle Green

KESWICK (Cumberland)
The Archway Antiques
17 John St, 842

J Young & Son
16 Main St, 156

KETTERING (Northants)
C W Ward (Antiques)
Deene House, 40 Lower St

KETTLESING (Yorks)
J M & E Rawson-Lax
Willow Brook, Birstwith 475

KEW GREEN (Surrey)
Kew Green Antiques
11 The Green, 940 3987

KIDDERMINSTER (Worcs)
J & D Bamber Ltd
9–10 Comberton Rd, 5731
Downtons
91 Coventry St, 2788

KINGS CAPEL (Hereford)
Castle Pool Antiques
Kings Caple Ct, Carey 666
The Hereford Gallery
Kings Caple Ct, Carey 666

KINGS LANGLEY (Herts)
Langley Antiques
15–17 High St, 4417

KINGS LYNN (Norfolk)
Eva Baird
4 Saturday Market Pl, 3931
J D & C P Bocking
23–32 Queen St, 2333
Marshalls
Railway Rd, 2592
Medina Gallery
Saturday Market Pl, 2416
Gifford B Page
2 New Conduit St, 2980
The Tower Gallery
Middleton Tower, Middleton 203
C Winlove
14 Purfleet St

KINGSBRIDGE (Devon)
Halsey & Son (Kingsbridge) Ltd
Boffin's Boft, Bowcombe Creek, 2440

KINGSTON (Hereford)
Boyne House (Kingston) Ltd
6 Bridge St, 223

KINGSTON-ON-THAMES (Surrey)
Kingston Antiques
138 London Rd, 2221
R G Rummery Ltd
14 Kingston Hill, 5999

KINGSWORTHY (Hants)
Kingsworthy Antiques
London Road, Winchester 5595

125

KINVER (Worcs)

Holbein House Antiques
31 High St, 2650

KIRKBY LONSDALE (Westmorland)

Mitchelgate Antiques
2 Mitchelgate, 422
Town End Antiques
16 Main St

KNARESBOROUGH (Yorks)

Joan Eyles
24 High St, 2391
House of Antiques, Arts & Crafts
48 High St, 3317
P Kirk
6 and 8 Bond End, 2041
Charles F Thorpe
Roughstones, Forest Moor Rd, 3004
(by appt)

KNOWLE (Warks)

Chester House Antiques
2149
A T Silvester & Sons Ltd
The Olde House, Station Rd, 5171

KNUTSFORD (Cheshire)

Cranford Galleries
10 King St, 3646
John Curbishley
19 King St, 3430
John Duxfield Antiques
15 Brook St, 3455
Arthur Lee
Hollingford House, Toft Rd, 3134
Anderson Slater Antiques
8 King St, 2917
Michael Wisehall Antiques
7 Minshull St, 4901

LACOCK (Wilts)

Christopher Truman Antiques
8 Church St

LAMBERHURST (Kent)

Antiques
Tile House, School Hill, 360

LANCASTER (Lancs)

C Craig
55 Penny St, 66366
Mitchelgate Antiques
54 North Rd, 66050

LANGPORT (Som)

The Shop
Picts Hill, 442

LANGTON GREEN (Kent)

The Antique Shop
Langton Rd

LAVENHAM (Suffolk)

Angel Corner Antiques
17 Market Pl, 474
Little Cottage Antiques
81–83 High St
R McCausland-White
The Antique Shop, 4 High St, 356
T Smith
31–32 High St, 349
Straddles Antiques
Church St, 518

LAVERTON (Glos)

Laverton Antiques
Stanton 203

LEAMINGTON SPA (Warks)

Charles Antiques Ltd
Blackdown Mill, 22614
Ivanna's Antiques
George St, 24334
Royal Leamington Antiques
74 Upper Holly Walk, 23068
Percy F Wale Ltd
32 Regent St, 21288

LECHLADE (Glos)

John Havinden
Greville Manor, 267
Lucy Cleave

LEDBURY (Hereford)

G V A & H Seccombe-Hett
4 So ꞌnd, 2956
Tudor ꞏ .se Antiques
42 The Homend, 2973

LEEDS (Yorks)

Alexandra Galleries
30 Park Cross St, 22719
L P Balmforth & Son
31–33 Merrion St, 27583
Bulmers Antiques
226 Harrogate Rd, 681785
Gerald Dimery
154 Shadwell Lane, Moortown, 682777
J Feather
120 Gledhow Valley Rd, 684915
Nat Gaunt & Co
70 North St, 28847
Grand Antiques
51d New Briggate, 25110
Hamilton Antiques
110 North St, 28691
Henson's Antiques
7a Chapel Pl, North Lane, Headingley,
51914
L Kelvin Antiques
138 North St, 686582
Olympic Galleries
72 Woodhouse Lane, 684556
Smiths Antiques
17 St Michael's Lane, Headingley, 55461

P D & S Solden
65 Mabgate, 22229
Lisa Taylor Antiques
110a North St, 26145 and Rawdon
3617 (priv)
T L Thirkill
2a Green Lane, 639303 (Tues only or
by appt)
Walinet
43 Chapeltown Rd, 656699
Warwick Antiques
234 Roundhay Rd
Windsor House Antiques
210 Woodhouse Lane, 23451
Windsor House Antiques
Stainbeck Corner, Chapeltown,
629053
L A & J Witty
233 Harehills Lane, 623127
Woodruff Antiques
164a Roundhay Rd and 165 Harehills
Lane, 629733

LEEDSTOWN
(Cornwall)
A W Glasby & Son Antiques
303

LEEK (Staffs)
Antiques and Objets d'Art of Leek
71 St Edwards St, 587
Norman Grosvenor
Britannia Bldgs, Gladstone St, 4475
Heath of Leek
Overton Bank House, 3096
Mrs Joyce Smallman
1 Clerk Bank, 3062

LEICESTER
John Desmond Antiques
80–82 Welford Rd, 59465
Kathleen d'Offay
46–48 Waterloo St, 59567
Esme Dunn Antiques
2 Paigle Rd, Aylestone, 831854
Forest Lodge Antiques
135 East Park Rd, 56616
J Green & Son
22 Melton Rd, 61495
Walter Moores & Son
89 Wellington St, 24416

J A Morrison (Firearms) Ltd
153 Scraptoft Lane, Thurnby 3750
G Novakovic
54 St Stephens Rd, 28977
Withers of Leicester
142a London Rd, 58739
J E Wrightson
135 East Park Rd, 706621

LEIGH-ON-SEA (Essex)
Antiques
125 Rectory Grove, Southend
78080

LEIGHTON BUZZARD
(Beds)
A Timms Antiques
61 North St

LEISTON (Suffolk)
Cross Street Antiques

LEOMINSTER
(Hereford)
J A Bishop
Shaftesbury House, 2050
J N Eddy
22 Etnam St, 2813
C Faulkner
5 Bridge St, 2469
W & A Garman
Marsh House, Bridge St, 2946
(trade only)
Leonard Tilston
25 Broad St

LEWES (Sussex)
Coombe House Antiques
Malling St, 3862
De Montfort Antiques
10 Station Rd, 4778
Friars Walk Antiques
21 Friars Walk, 2549
Stephen Moore Ltd
Castle Pl, 166 High St, 4158 and
103 High St
C Roy Newton
Ye Olde Shoppe, Cliffe Corner,
2455

127

LICHFIELD (Staffs)
The Little Gallery Antiques
Jack and Robert Whitney, 19 Dam St,
4418

LIMPLEY STOKE
(Wilts)
Richard de Blangy
The Manor House, Lower Limpley
Stoke, 2163

LIMPSFIELD
(Surrey)
Ann Gray Antiques
The Antique Shop, Oxted 3836

LINCOLN
Michael Brewer
16 and 18 Steep Hill, 24773
C Cottam & Son
Jews House, 15 Strait, 25616
Alfred Dovey
25 Steep Hill, 25839
The Spinning Wheel
39 Steep Hill, 22463
Jacqueline Stevenson
8 Bailgate, 27022
A E Syson & Son
13 Steep Hill, 26201
James Usher & Son Ltd
263 High St, 27547
E E Wallis
Aaron the Jew's House, 46 Steep Hill,
28996

LINDFIELD (Sussex)
Lindfield Antiques
99 High St, 2483
Arthur Thomas
4 Denmans Lane, Ardingly 382

LINTON (Essex)
A E Satchell Antiques
57 High St, 754 861

LISS (Hants)
David Clark
143 Station Rd, Liphook 3277
C H Dunkley
The Malt House, West Liss, 3104
Greentree Antiques
West Liss, 3328

LITTLE BEALINGS
(Suffolk)
Christopher Morley
Heath Cottages, Kesgrave 4208

LITTLEBURY
(Essex)
The Old Carpenters Arms
Saffron Walden 2546

LITTLEHAMPTON
(Sussex)
Corner Cupboard Antiques
88 Lyminster Rd, 752
Maurice Knight
41 High St, 6583

LITTLE MAPLESTEAD
(Essex)
Bay Window Antiques
Hampers, Halstead 2159

LITTLE PENGETHLEY
(Hereford)
Miss Gwyneth Preece
off A49 Ross to Hereford

LIVERPOOL (Lancs)
Boodle & Dunthorne Ltd
Lord St, MAR 2525
Boydell Galleries
15 Castle St, 236 3256
Leonard of Liverpool
69 Bold St, ROY 8462
John Maggs
114 Bold St, ROY 2742
E Pryor & Son
110 London Rd, ROY 1361
C Rosenberg
The Antique Shop, 12 Exchange St East,
236 1516
Pat Stone Antiques
12 South John St, 236 1696

LLANDOVERY
(Carmarthens)
Antique Shop
7 Kings Rd

LLANDUDNO (Caernarvon)
The Antique Shop
24 Vaughan St, 75575
Joan M Cash
8 Clonmel St, 75425
C & H Wartski
93 Mostyn St, 76191

LLANFAIR CAEREINION
(Montgomery)
The Rocking Horse
205

LLANWARNE
(Nr Hereford)
Llanwarne Court
Wormelow 385

LOCKERBIE (Scotland)
Antiques
110 High St, 2646

LONG COMPTON (Warks)
John Faulkner
Wedgwood Cott, 233

LONG HANBOROUGH (Oxon)
Ann Winchester
Hanborough Antiques, 127 Main Rd,
Freeland 484

LONG MELFORD (Suffolk)
Armstrong Antiques
Hall St, 281
Bassetts House Antiques
opp Bull Hotel, 464 (pm only)
Magill Antiques
Chestnut House, 484

LONG STRATTON (Norfolk)
The Antique Shop
by Barclay's Bank, 479
The Georgian Shop
Norwich 24495

LONG SUTTON (Lincs)
Seven Feathers
15 London Rd, 2244

LOOE (Cornwall)
Tony Martin
Archway Antiques, Fore St, 2734

LOSTWITHIEL (Cornwall)
Mary Farrant Antiques
22 Queen St, 227
(closed Monday)

LOUGHBOROUGH (Leics)
Colconda
16 Leicester Rd, 61906
Lowe of Loughborough Ltd
37–40 Church Gate, 2554

LOWDHAM (Notts)
Lowdham Antiques
Gunthorpe Rd, 3306

LOWESTOFT (Suffolk)
The Antique Shop
31 High St, 3380
Antiques Decorious
50 High St
Clock Antiques
138 High St, 2945

LOXWOOD (Sussex)
Deanery Antiques
Linden House, 223

LUDLOW (Shrops)
Broadgate Antiques
Oriel House, 49 Broad St, 2699
Emporos
27 Bull Ring 3392
D Glasford
White Lodge, Mill St

Mina Maxwell
22–23 Bull Ring, 2884
Paul Smith
10 Church St, 2666
Tamberlane House
Buttercross, 2666

LUSTLEIGH (Devon)
Wreyland Manor Antiques
326

LYMINGTON (Hants)
Corfield of Lymington Ltd
120 High Street, 3532
F & L Fruitnight
5–9 New St, 2869
The Furniture House
Ashley Lane, 2846
R G Smith
26 Gosport St, 2666

LYNDHURST (Hants)
Antique Galleries
25 High St, 259
Lita Kaye
13 High St, 2337
Manor Farm Antiques
Minstead, Cadnam 3126
Old Pump House
20 High St, 2137

LYNMOUTH (Devon)
Lyncliff Antiques
Watersmeet Rd, Lynton 3241

MACCLESFIELD (Cheshire)
Copperfields
38–40 Jordangate, Green Hills 2661
Mr &Mrs Dabinett
The Antique Shop, Mill Lane
P Bracegirdle
2 Chester Rd
The Singing Bird
1 George St West, Greenhills
3467

MACHYNLLETH (Montgomery)
Robert Gwatkin
Maengwyn St, 2336
Colin Hughes
36 Penrallt St, 2363
G M Hughes
6 Penrallt St, 2053

MAENTWROG (Merioneth)
The Old Post Office
Tanybwlch, 209

129

MAIDENHEAD (Berks)

E T Biggs & Sons Ltd
26–32 High St, 26363
W & E Edgar Ltd
92 Bridge Rd, 23507

MAIDSTONE (Kent)

Peter Bonnert
20 The Broadway, 55610
Cheshire Martin Ltd
21–25 Earl St, 56976
Mrs M Turk
4 Clarendon Pl, King St, 51284
(closed Wed)
Michael Winch
Boughton Monchelsea Pl, 43120

MALMESBURY (Wilts)

Joyce Cherrington
Market Cross
Keyford Galleries
Avon Mills, 2203

MALPAS (Cheshire)

Stewart Evans
Church View, 214 (trade only)

MALTON (Yorks)

Baccarat
1 Savile St, 3434
D & M Lindley
69 Commercial St, Norton, 3220

MALVERN (Worcs)

The Cedars Antiques
36 Bellevue Terr, 61173
Michael Milburn
45 Worcester Rd, 4620

MANCHESTER (Lancs)

Arden Gallery
58 Dene Rd, Didsbury,
Manchester 21,
Didsbury 9795
The Armourer's Shop
61 Bridge St, 061 790 2484
The Connoisseur
528 Wilmslow Rd, Withington,
Didsbury 2504
The Four Lamps
50 Cannon St, Manchester 4,
BLA 2420

Gay's Antiques
778 Wilmslow Rd, Didsbury,
Manchester 20, Didsbury 7315
G Glass Ltd
40 King St, BLA 1321
Lapwing Antiques (Derek L Jones Ltd)
103 Lapwing Lane, West Didsbury,
Manchester 20, 061 445 8340
Frank Wine & Son Ltd
71 Barton Arcade, BLA 9087

MARKET DEEPING (Lincs)

The Old Curiosity Shop
29 Church St, 3193

MARKET DRAYTON (Shrops)

A J Jones
8 Stafford St, Moreton-in-Hales 222

MARKET HARBOROUGH (Leics)

George Burgess
6–7 The Square, 2168
Molly Rowen
35 High St, 2726

MARKET WEIGHTON (Yorks)

Houghton Hall Antiques
Hough Hall, Cliffe Rd, 3234

MARLBOROUGH (Wilts)

Dormy House Antiques
43 Kingsbury St, 2703

MARLOW (Bucks)

Bishop (Marlow) Ltd
8 and 10 West St, 3936
Regency House Antiques
48 Chapel St, 2792
Walker Antiques
59 High St, 2882
Willow Antiques
40 Chapel St, 5376

MARSHFIELD (Glos)

The Old Inn
Market Pl, 245 (by appt)

MAYFIELD (Sussex)
Metropolitan Arms Co Ltd
3288

MELTON MOWBRAY (Leics)
Wylton Antiques Ltd
High St, 2249

MENAI BRIDGE (Anglesey)
Robert Brown Antiques
30 High St, 498

MERSTHAM (Surrey)
Charles Mundy
30 High St, 3443

MEVAGISSEY (Cornwall)
Lord Douglas Gordon
Portmellon, 3235

MIDDLESBROUGH (Yorks)
Antiques Shop
1a Victoria Rd (closes 4 pm)
R S Richardson
1 Newton St, 3064

MIDDLETON (Norfolk)
The Tower Gallery
Middleton Tower

MIDDLE WALLOP (Hants)
Kate Appleton Antiques
Turnpike Cott, 341
Roger & Francesca Wilson
The Old George, 422

MIDHURST (Sussex)
Eagle House Antiques
Church Hill, 2718
Hill House Antiques
Church Hill House, 841
H W Keil Ltd
Knockhundred House, 3133
The Lantern
3 South St
St Anne's Hill House Antiques
2746
The White House
South St, 2024
The White Panther
North St, 2720

MILEHAM (Norfolk)
Henry Merckel
Treasures Gallery

MILFORD (Surrey)
The Refectory
1234

MILFORD-ON-SEA (Hants)
Etcetera
57 High St, 2386
Trivia
27 High St, 2748

MODBURY (Devon)
Mr & Mrs Pittis
3 Broad St, 426

MONMOUTH
The Old Coach House
14 Church St, 2532
Kathleen Frost Antiques
8 Priory St
Dorothy Silvester Antiques
Worcester Lodge, 105-107 Monnow St,
2350

MONTACUTE (Som)
The Antique Shop
17 The Borough Sq, Martock 2364

MORETONHAMPSTEAD (Devon)
The Maltsters' House
413
The Old Brass Kettle
334

MORETON-IN-THE-MARSH (Glos)
R G Baker
High St, 763
George Bolam
Creswyke House, High St, 751
The Cottage Antique Shop
High St
The Centuries Antiques
High St, 448
T N Hill & Son
High St
The Little Window
High St
Old Parsonage Cottage Antiques
Church St, 492

MORPETH (Northumberland)
Beeswing Antiques
The Beeswing, 93 Newgate St, 2424
H Bellerby
69 Bridge St, 636

MOUNTNESSING (Essex)
Hampton House
309-311 Roman Rd, Brentwood 7525
(mainly trade)

MOUNTSORREL (Leics)
Gordon & Mavis Mee
3 Market Pl, Rothley 2037

MUCH WENLOCK (Shrops)
Abbey Antiques Ltd
Bridgnorth Rd, 330
Crossbow Antiques
12 High St, Worfield 641
Malthouse Antiques
467

MUNSLOW (Shrops)
Millichope Antiques
651

NAILSWORTH (Glos)
Witch Ball Antiques
Church St, 2640

NANTWICH (Cheshire)
Antiques
128 Hospital Rd, 64567
Winifred Pearson
63-67 Welsh Row, 65872
Townwell House Antiques
52 Welsh Row, 65953

NETHERAVON (Wilts)
White Owl Collectors' Cottage
396 (Fri, Sat, Sun or by appt)

NEWARK-ON-TRENT
Frederick J McCarthy
14 Castle Gate, 4798

NEWBOLD-ON-STOUR
(Warks)
A A Whitcombe
The Grange Antiques

NEW BUCKENHAM
(Norfolk)
Joan Fitz Patrick
Corner House, 372

NEWBURY (Berks)
Aubrey J Coleman of Newbury
Hunters Lodge, London Rd, 552 and at
The Antique Galleries, 104, Northbrook
St, 552
M Jarvis (Antiques) Ltd
The High House, Oxford St, 249
The Kennet Gallery
76 Northbrook St, 2974
Margaret Metcalf
16 Oxford St, 801
Stuart & Turner Ltd
Clarendon House, London Rd, 1435

NEWBY BRIDGE (Lancs)
Townhead Antiques
321

NEWCASTLE-UPON-TYNE
(Northumberland)
Corbitt & Hunter
3 St Nicholas Bldgs, Newcastle 1,
21784/21036

Cradlewell Antiques
244 Jesmond Rd, Newcastle 2, 810691
Roger Freer Antiques
16 Shakespeare St, 26765
Hawthorn Cottage Antiques
8 Hawthorn Rd, Gosforth, 54836
Owen Humble
11-12 Clayton Rd, Jesmond, Newcastle
2, 812661
N Jewett
639-643 Durham Rd, Low Fell,
Gateshead 9, Low Fell, 877636
Reid & Sons Ltd
23-27 Blackett St, 21366 and
126 Grainger St, 20673
Ian A Robertson
Surtees House, 41 Sandhill, 22921
H M Sidney
12 Saville Row, Newcastle 1, 26702
J G Trench
3 Church Rd, Gosforth, Newcastle 3,
Gosforth 55620
Westgate Antiques
283 Westgate Rd, 24951

NEWENT (Glos)
The Antique Shop
Church St, 325
Owl Antiques
High St, 400

NEWMARKET (Suffolk)
Ashley House Antiques
Old Station Rd, 3979
Savage & Sturgeon
Queensbury Lodge, High St, 2751

NEW MILTON (Hants)
Lindsay Antiques
Lymington Rd, 955

NEWNHAM-ON-SEVERN
(Glos)
Castle Antiques
The Paddocks, 335
Geoffrey Kenyon-May
Green Acre, Broad Oak
Hill House Antiques
High St, 309 (open 11-4)

NEWPORT (Essex)
Jennys Broom Antiques
High St, Brent Pelham 341
The Little Owl Antiques
High St, 623
Newport Antiques
High St, 321

NEWPORT
(Isle of Wight)
Braunstone Galleries
Braunstone House, Lugley St, 2756
A King
34 Lugley St, 2481

Rembrandt Galleries
73 High St, 2878

NEWPORT (Monmouth)
Antiques
82–84 Chepstow Rd, 59935
Antiques
79 High St, 62303
D S Hutchings
210 Chepstow Rd, 71944
The Variety Box (Antiques)
21 and 21a Caerleon Rd

NEWPORT (Shropshire)
Fox & Dawes
60 Upper Bar, Open-Gate 2668
St Mary's Antiques

NEWPORT PAGNELL (Bucks)
The Gift Shop
16 St John St, 761

NEWTON ABBOT (Devon)
Forde House Antiques Ltd
Torquay Rd, 4690
Meade House
57 East St, 3353
Lydia Scott (Antiques)
(Mr & Mrs F J Page), 6 St Pauls Rd, 5653

NEWTOWN (Montgomery)
Severn Antiques
11–12 Severn St, 265

NORTH CURRY (Som)
Sedgemoor Antiques
Brook Farm, 444

NORTHALLERTON (Yorks)
Antiques
Zetland St, 2886 (closed Thurs)

NORTHAMPTON
Cave's
111 Kettering Rd, 38278 and Regent
House, Royal Terr, 37992

NORTHCHAPEL (Sussex)
Antiques
379

NORTHCHURCH (Herts)
Northchurch Antiques
53 Northchurch High St,
Berkhamsted 6355

NORTHIAM (Sussex)
Northiam Antiques
3252

NORTHLEACH (Glos)
M E Rivers-Moore
West End, Northleach, 369

NORTH SHIELDS (Northumberland)
Centurion Antiques
13 Union St

NORTON (Suffolk)
Cottage Antiques
Blinkbourne, Elmswell 404

NORWICH (Norfolk)
Antiques & Paintings
25a Tombland, 24771
The Art Gallery
Bramerton Lane, Framingham Pigot
Harold Beazor
30 Elm Hill, 24495
Arthur Brett & Sons Ltd
42 St Giles St, 28171
Flint House Art Gallery
34 Elm Hill, 26159
Donald Hannent
The Barn, 12 School Lane, Sprowston
48333
Henry Levine
1 Castle St, 28709
Mandell's Gallery
Elm Hill, 26892
Paston House Gallery
20 Elm Hill, 21260
Rackheath Hall
Rackheath Pk, Salhouse 326
Maud Suffling Gift Antiques
IIa St Benedicts, 29231 and 45801
R Townshend
29 Elm Hill, 26592
R Watling
40 St Giles St

NOTTINGHAM (Notts)
Antiques
34 Sherwood St
Antiques
15-17 Mansfield Rd, 43160
Antiques
19 Mansfield Rd, 42712
Maurice Barrow
19 Mansfield Rd
Bonfiglioli (Nottm) Ltd
Milbie House, 33 Pilcher Gate, 51690
(by appt)
Peter Corton
86 Derby Rd, 46497
Hillstonia Antiques
312 Nottingham Rd, Selston, Pinxton
469
Leslie Jones Antiques Ltd
80 Derby Rd
N Kemp
89-91 Derby Rd, 47055
Langale Ltd
213 Mansfield Rd, 44764
David Potter
258 Sherwood St, 47911

133

J Shine
239 Mansfield Rd, 47770
Thomas Turner
265 Mansfield Rd, 45333
Frances M Wardle
3 Owthorpe Rd, Cotgrave, Cotgrave 214

ODIHAM (Hants)
Anthony Bird
Chevertons, Potbridge, 2450
Odiham Antiques
The Old House, High St, 2557
Wessex House Antiques
High St, 2237

OKEHAMPTON (Devon)
S & S (Antiques) Ltd
5 West St, 2452

OLDHAM (Lancs)
The Curio Shop
538 Huddersfield Rd, 061 633 3078

OLNEY (Bucks)
The Antique Shop
7 Market Pl, 425

OSBOURNEY (Lincs)
Vincent Wood
Audley House, Culverthorpe 251
(trade only)

OSWESTRY (Shropshire)
Barbara Jameson Antiques
92 Willow St, 3688

OTLEY (Yorks)
Bowes Antiques
3 Charles St, 2647
Chevin Antiques
Westgate, Guiseley 3404
Daffil Antiques
32-36 Bondgate and 13 Crossgates,
3536 or Leeds 680919
H & M Suttle
16 Market Pl and 1 Bridge St, 2313

OTTERY ST MARY (Devon)
Georgian House Antiques
13 Silver St, 2637

OUSDEN (Suffolk)
Quality Wood
Cropley Grove, 226

OVERTON (Hants)
Anton Galleries
XXIa High St, 406

OXFORD
The Antiquary
50 St Giles, 59875
P Audley Miller
48 High St, 47952

Bonfiglioli
104 The High, 42590
Reginald Davis
34 High St, 48347
The East Gate Gallery
71 High St, 43808
Halcrow
30 Little Clarendon St, St Giles
C John
36 High St, 44197
A & J Stuart Mobey
38 Little Clarendon St, 58853
North Parade Antiques
75 Banbury Rd, 59816
Oseney Town Antiques
76 Bridge St, Oseney 40455
Payne & Son (Goldsmiths) Ltd
131 High St, 43787
St Clements Antiques
11-12 St Clements, 41904 and 105
Bullingdon Rd, 42474
Sanders
104 The High St, 42590
The Ship St Antique Gallery
5 Ship St, 48130
White's Antiques
102 Walton St, 58596

PAIGNTON (Devon)
Ward's Antique Shop
30 Hyde Rd, 59725

PAINSWICK (Glos)
Antiques Gallery
St Mary's St
Katherine Christophers
Kings Mill, Painswick 3328
Hammand Antiques
Friday St, 2310

PANGBOURNE (Berks)
Passers Buy
3 High St, 2662

PARKGATE (Cheshire)
The Green Bottle
The Parade, Neston 2823

PAULERSPURY (Northants)
The Antique Galleries
Watling St, 238

PEMBURY (Kent)
The Old House
30 Hastings Rd, 2807

PENN (Bucks)
The Country Furniture Shop
3 Hazlemere Rd, 2244
Francis Wigram of Penn
3266

PENRITH (Cumberland)
Antiques
39 Duke St, 3099
Antiques of Penrith
4 Corney Sq, 2801
Harper's Antiques
Temple Sowerby, Kirkby Thore 359
Hamish Kirsop Antiques
Lowthwaite, Matterdale, Glenridding 343
(by appt)

PENSHURST (Kent)
Penshurst Antiques
Bridge House, 209

PENZANCE (Cornwall)
Antiques
48 and 68 Market Jew St, 3013 4388
Commander England Ltd
26 Causewayhead and 57 Adelaide St, 3933
F A Wooldridge
1-2 Alverton Terr

PERSHORE (Worcs)
Mercy Jeboult
Perrot House, 17 Bridge St, 301

PERTH (Scotland)
Wm Fettes & Son
15 Atholl St, 21382
Thomas Love & Sons Ltd
51, 53 and 62 South St, 24111

PETERBOROUGH (Northants)
Potter
293 and 719 Lincoln Rd, Millfield 2487 68216
Studio Antiques
42 Cowgate, 4394

PETERSFIELD (Hants)
Antiques
38 Dragon St
The Barn
Station Rd, 2958
Dragon Antiques
9 Dragon St, 2570
Durston's Antiques
4 College St, 194

Morris Nash Antiques
36 Dragon St, 2688
The Petersfield Galleries
11 Charles St, 2215
Eleanor Pudner Antiques
1 Heath Rd, 1030
Renaissance Studio
35 Lavant St, 3104

PETWORTH (Sussex)
Boss Antiques
Lombard St
C Denman & Son
East St, 3179
John G Morris Ltd
Market Sq, 2305
John Rowe
Market Sq
Ernest Streeter & Daughter
Clock House, Church St, 2239

PEVENSEY (Sussex)
The Old Mint House
Westham 337

PEWSEY (Wilts)
Rupert Gentle
The Manor House, Milton Lilbourne 3344

PICKERING (Yorks)
John Hague
Central Furniture Hall, Bridge St, 2829
C Duncan Taylor
The Shambles, 46 Market Pl, 2160

PINBROOK (Hants)
Peter Worley
54 London Rd, Waterlooville 3031

PLUMTREE (Notts)
Plumtree Antiques & Curios
Main St, 2190
Antiques
Market Sq

PLYMOUTH (Devon)
Alvin
148 Union St, 65628 and Jamaica House, Barbican, 67990
R & M Andrade Ltd
50 Southside St, 64203

135

Antiques
The Island House, The Barbican, 60946
and **Antiques**
34 New St, The Barbican
Benton & Coleman
29 Southside St and 202 Exeter St,
66522
J Moorland Coon Ltd
Townsend Hill, 68920
Galaxy Arts Ltd
38 New St, Barbican, 67842

PLYMPTON (Devon)
Reg & Muriel Andrade Ltd
3, 7 and 8 Boringdon Villas,
37952

PONTYPRIDD (Glam)
Bown's Antique Stores
10 Sardis Rd, 2170

POOLE (Dorset)
Miss Evelyn Harris Antiques
7 Thames St, 2977

PORLOCK (Som)
Eric E Fordred Ltd
205

PORTISHEAD (Som)
The Curiosity Shop
61 Woodhill Rd, 2547

PORTMEIRION (Merioneth)
Angel Arcade
within private grounds entrance fee
about 7s 6d, Penrhyndeudraeth
228 338

PORTSMOUTH (Hants)
Feakins Antiques
41 Shadwell Rd, 63158
Leslies
107 Fratton Rd, 25952
J Nicholl McKay
251 Highland Rd, Eastley, 35191
S H Mitchell
25 Commercial Rd, 27377
New Road Stores
123 New Rd, 63044
Ophir Antiques
295 London Rd, 07 056 0574
T Rolph
Nirvana Mansions, 14 Eastern Vill Rd,
33995
Wolf Antiques
18 Marmion Rd, 27454

POTTERSPURY (Northants)
Reindeer Antiques
Watling St, Yardley Gobion 607

PRESTATYN (Flints)
Owain Glyndwr Antiques
Greenmead, Meliden Rd, 2637 (trade
only)

PRESTON (Lancs)
Richard Bamber & Son Ltd
102-104 Friargate, 54352
Maurice Manning
The Old Corn Mill, Preston Rd, Alston,
Longridge 3505
Edward Nield
51 Church St, 55144
Frederick Treasure Ltd
Marsh Lane, 54414

PRINCES RISBOROUGH (Bucks)
Alscot Antiques
Alscot Lodge, 531

PULBOROUGH (Sussex)
Roy Barton
Myrtle Cottage, Codmore Hill, 2730
(trade only)
Mare Hill Antiques Ltd
Mare Hill, 2762 (closed Mon)
Vincent Antiques
50 Lower St, 2824

PULHAM MARKET (Norfolk)
The Old Bakery
218

PURBROOK (Hants)
Stanley Riddell
105 Park Ave

QUATFORD (Shrops)
Quatford Galleries Antiques
Bridgnorth 3213

QUENDON (Essex)
The Old Kings Head
Rickling 344

RAINFORD (Lancs)
Colin Stock
8 Mossborough Rd, 2246

RAMSGATE (Kent)
Norman Marks
23 Chapel Pl, Thanet 53444
Smugglers Barn Antiques
Pegwell Rd, Thanet 52948

READING (Berks)
The Antiquary
29 London Rd, 54350
Antiques
49 London St, 53962
Bracher & Sydenham Ltd
26–30a Queen Victoria St, 53724

John E Davis
14 Wokingham Rd, 63108
S J Evans
69 London St, 50968
L J Kingston & Son
27 London Rd, 51131
J J Nelson
92 London St, 57595
Gordon Sutcliffe Ltd
36 Castle St, 50148
The Variety Shop
209 Caversham Rd, 55620

REDBOURN (Herts)
Spinning Wheel Antiques
48 High St, 0582 85 2160

REDDITCH (Worcs)
Capella Antiques
124 Evesham St, 2408
The Old Coach House
St Leonard's Grange, Beoley, 2145

REDHILL (Surrey)
Wakeman Bros
78 Brighton Rd, 895
S Warrender Ltd
57 High St, 64006

REIGATE (Surrey)
J M Powell
45 Church St, 44111
Reigate Galleries
45 Bell St, 46055

RETFORD (Notts)
F C Dixon
54 Bridgegate, 2660

RHOS-ON-SEA (Denbigh)
Shelagh Hyde
11 Rhos Rd, Colwyn Bay 48879

RICHMOND (Surrey)
Antiquaria and Little Gallery
15 Paved Court
The Antique Market
74 Richmond Hill
Antiques
24 Richmond Hill
John Barry
20a Richmond Hill, 589 3042
J Clapper
5 Richmond Hill, 1798
Court Antiques
Brewers Lane, 0515
De Grandcourt
12 Paved Court, The Green, 940 7815
Richmond Hill Antiques
12 Richmond Hill
Richmond Hill Gallery
39 Richmond Hill
C Vaughan Hoad
17 Sheen Common Dr, 876 4718 (by appt)

L E King Antiques
13 The Green
Loco
4–6 Paradise Rd, 6176

RICHMOND (Yorks)
K Agar
9 Castle Hill, 3285
Araxie Love
15 and 47 Newbiggin, 3278

RINGWOOD (Hants)
J I Cropley
Antiques, 80 Christchurch Rd, 2973
Duck Island Antiques
Duck Island Lane, 2587
M & R Garman
56 Christchurch Rd, 2377
Matchbox Antiques
132 Christchurch Rd
Netherbrook Antiques
85 Christchurch Rd, 2062

RIPLEY (Surrey)
Broadway Villa Antiques
High St, 3415
Anthony Cooper
67 High St, 2333
W G Ellard
The Green Cottage, Portsmouth Rd,
2396 (trade mainly)
A E Gould & Sons (Antiques) Ltd
186 High St, 2318
John Hill
Elm Tree House, 3131
Manor House
3350

RIPON (Yorks)
J W Bentall
The City Arms, High Skellgate,
2551
W Hemsworth & Son
8 Fishergate, 2113

ROBERTSBRIDGE (Sussex)
Agramens Antiques
56 High St, 308
De Montfort Antiques
High St
The Grange Antiques
The Grange, High St, 577
The Old Forge
362
Robertsbridge House Antiques
Robertsbridge House, High St, 291
Peter S Westbury
25–27 High St, 226

ROBIN HOOD'S BAY (Yorks)
Discovery Antiques Ltd
The Quay

ROLVENDEN (Kent)
Falstaff Antiques
234

ROMSEY (Hants)
Abbey Antiques
Middle Bridge St, 3068
Olive Parry Ltd
15 Middle Bridge St, 3356

ROOKLEY (Isle of Wight)
Malt House Antiques
Niton Rd, Chillerton 265

ROSS-ON-WYE (Hereford)
M J Cooke
Church St
Mrs K Frost
Colgarron, Goodrich, Symonds Yat 256
Tony Howell
23 Brookent St, 3036
The Old Court House Antiques
53 High St, 3010
Owl Antiques
High St, 3836
Howard Vaughan Ltd
Gloucester Rd, 2241
White Horses
14 Gloucester Rd, Lydbrook 254

ROSSET (Denbighs)
Times Past Antiques
Rosset Cottage, 516

ROTHERHAM (Yorks)
John Mason (Rotherham) Ltd
36 High St, 2311
George Wright (Rotherham) Ltd
The Crofts, 3871

ROTTINGDEAN (Sussex)
Trade Winds
15a Little Crescent, Brighton 31177

ROWLANDS CASTLE (Hants)
D Dobson
3 Links Lane, 507

ROYSTON (Cambs)
P N Hardiman
Baldock St, 2172

RUFFORD (Lancs)
Bower House
Liverpool Rd, 274

RUGELEY (Staffs)
Brereton Hall
Brereton, 2476
Eveline Winter
1 Wolseley Rd, 3259

RUNCORN (Cheshire)
B Braverman
58 High St, 2529

RUSTINGTON (Sussex)
Mayes
8 Sea Lane

RUTHIN (Denbigh)
Grosvenor Galleries
Wynnstay Rd, 3126

RYDE (Isle of Wight)
Joan Burke
11 Union St, 3115
Hayters
20 Cross St, 3795
L J Jeffrey
95 High St, 3224
Mitchell Bros
16 Cross St, 3436

RYE (Sussex)
Charlotte Adams
35 The Mint, 2065
Bragge & Sons
Landgate House, 3358
George & Son
Down Pass, High St
The Lion Galleries
2208
The Old Hall Gallery Ltd
Iden, Iden 304
Rye Antiques
93 High St, 2259
Strand Antiques
3112
Vercasson
Old Oast Pl, Icklesham,
Icklesham 232

ST ALBANS (Herts)
Antelope Antiques
19–20 George St, 57798
Crispin
37 Holywell Hill, 53230
Dunnings Antiques
(Mrs Christopher Sykes)
58–62 Holywell Hill, 56741
Josephine Grahame-Ballin
21 George St, 56069
James
11 George St, 56996
W J Lomas
13 Holywell Hill, Hepplewhite House,
57300
F E Norwood Ltd
23 Holywell Hill, 55955
Charles Perry
105 Holywell Hill, 53487
Pillers
15 and 21 Holywell Hill, 60864

ST ANNES-ON-SEA (Lancs)

Georgian House
37 Wood St, 23029
Spinning Wheel Antiques
Major & Mrs C M Yates, 12 St Albans
Rd, 24187

ST BRIAVELS (Glos)

Bigsweir House
282

ST HELIER (Jersey)

William Fox
41 New St, Jersey Central 24436

ST IVES (Cornwall)

Figurehead
Fore St, 6428
Marjorie Parr
Wills Lane, Market Pl, 5723

ST LEONARDS-ON-SEA

Hastings Antiques
59-61 Norman Rd, Hastings 28561

ST MARGARETS (Herts)

Manor Antiques
43 Hoddesdon Rd, Stanstead Abbots 357

SAFFRON WALDON (Essex)

Julia Bennett
82 High St, 2016
Norfolk Antiques
16 Market Row, 2170
Sunn Inn Antiques
Church St, 2685
Turpin Antiques
9 Market Pl
R B Walkyier & Son
17 High St

SALE (Cheshire)

The Antique Shop
183 Cross St, Manchester 4753
Eureka Antiques
18 Northenden Rd, 061 962 5629

SALFORD (Lancs)

Frith's
208 Chapel St, Blackfriars 5666

SALISBURY (Wilts)

Beaches of Salisbury
7 High St, 3801
D & M Beer
14 Winchester St, 4932
Anne Davenport Antiques
61 Milford St, 6905
Dolphin Galleries
53 St Ann St and 119 Dolphin St, 22842

Ian G Hastie
46 St Ann St, 22957
E G Hayes
69a Brown St, 2303
The Joiners Hall
St Ann St, 22842
Patrick Mullins
5 St John St, 2570
New St Antique Trading Co
1 New St, 5566
Rogerson Antiques
60 St Ann St, 3841
Salisbury Galleries
81 Milford St, 5545
Thurston
7 St John St, 22677
White Owl Collectors' Cottage
Netheravon, Netheravon 396

SANDWICH (Kent)

Mead Antiques
5 King St, 2193
James Porter
5 Potter St, 2218

SAWBRIDGEWORTH (Herts)

Quinneys
Walnut Tree Corner, 2393

SAXMUNDHAM (Suffolk)

Crown House Antiques
Somerville Galleries
2503

SCARBOROUGH (Yorks)

Boothman & Richardson
13 York Pl, 83
C H & D Burrows
15b St Thomas St, 61014
John More
37 Huntriss Row, 5819
Brian Thacker Antiques
160 Victoria Rd and Tudor House,
Marine Parade, St Nicholas Cliff
(April-October)
Raymond Warren
54 Ramshill Rd, 64974
Foley Whickham
4 Royal Hotel Shops, St Nicholas St, 3113
S Wilson
7 Valley Bridge Pde

SEAFORD (Sussex)

The Old House Antiques
High St, 2091

SELBORNE (Hants)

Bush House Antiques
339
The Old Bake House
302

139

SETTLE (Yorks)
Mary Milnthorpe Antiques
Market Place, 2331
Nanbooks
Devonshire House, Duke St,
3324

SEVENOAKS (Kent)
G E Field
27 London Rd, 52167
Malcolm Gardner
Bradbourne Farmhouse, Bradbourne
Vale Rd, 51311 (Horological books only)
Harrison of Sevenoaks
120 London Rd, 52104
Lime Tree Studio
Lime Tree Walk, 53150 (trade only)
Andrew Mair
44a High St, 55025

SHAFTESBURY (Dorset)
Roger and Jill Bichard
Cann Farm, Ringwood Rd, 2433

SHALDON (Devon)
The Olde Forge
76 Ringmore Rd, 2115

SHALFORD (Surrey)
H Meecham
2 Kings Rd, 61434

SHEFFIELD (Yorks)
Antiques
460-462 Glossop Rd
Artesque
886 Eccleshall Rd, Sheffield 11, 60576
Clifford Connelly
141 West St, 24422
G W Ford & Son Ltd
288-292 Glossop Rd, Sheffield 10,
22082
Jackson's Antiques
308-310 London Rd, Sheffield 2, 50235
and 223-227 Abbeydale Rd, Sheffield 7,
52101
A E Jameson & Co
257 Glossop Rd, 23846
Joses Antiques
405 Eccleshall Rd, Sheffield 11, 52214

SHELDWICH (Kent)
Lords Antiques
Faversham 2038

SHENFIELD (Essex)
The Corner House Antique Shop
5 Chelmsford Rd, Brentwood 2760

*A selection of bygones from
Deerstalker Antiques,
Whitchurch, Bucks*

SHEPTON MALLET (Som)
Grammar Galleries Ltd
The Old Grammar School House, 2563

SHERBORNE (Dorset)
Dodge & Son
Cheap St, 3487
Henry Durrant
Long St
Johnsons of Sherborne
South St
Newlands Antiques
Newland, 3464
Mrs Gavin Young
Spring House, Longburton, Holnest 240
(by appt)

SHERE (Surrey)
A G Askew & Son
Antiques, 2997
Vera Lloyd Antiques
Gomshall Mill, 2433

SHERINGHAM (Norfolk)
J J Harrold & Sons
Station App, 302
Mayfair House
60 Station Rd, 420

SHERSTON (Wilts)
Biggs of Sherston
High St, 368

SHILLINGSTONE (Dorset)
Peter Strowger
Main Rd A357, Child Okeford 231

SHIPLEY (Yorks)
W F & M C Barber
211 Bingley Rd, 58190
Bethell Antiques
149 Bradford Rd, Bradford 51318
Blenheim Antiques
283 Bradford Rd, Bradford 47673

SHIPSTON-ON-STOUR (Warks)
Shirley Brown
Tredington, 570
The Corner Cupboard
Mrs Jameson
Tredington (Thurs only or by appt, trade)
Henry Wigington
22 New St, 205

SHOREHAM (Sussex)
Leonard Goddard
358 and 364 Brighton Rd, 3841 (trade
only)

SHOTTERY (Warks)
The Web
Stratford 5517

SHOTTON (Flints)
Richard Nicholson
17-19 Chester Rd East, Connah's Quay
2626

SHREWSBURY (Shrops)
Antiques
Sun Tavern, Milk St, 55285
Howard Beach
10 St Julian's Friars, 54883
Enid Birch
3 Meadow Pl
N R Crow
182 Abbey Foregate, 6010
The Little Gallery
5 Wyle Cop, 52452
F C Manser & Son
21 Castle Gates, 51120
also at Meadow Pl
C J Pritchard
11 Fish St, 2854
Robinson & Co Ltd
9-10 The Square, 2919
R H V Tee & Son
131 Longden Coleham, 4565 (by appt)
G R Wycherley & Sons
42 High St, 2774

SKIPTON (Yorks)
Laycocks Antiques
Water St, 3247
Myers Galleries
Coach St, Skipton 2146

SNETTISHAM (Norfolk)
W L Tidd Antiques
435

SOHAM (Cambs)
Audraw Ltd
High St, 342

SOLIHULL (Warks)
B M Boyd
334 Stratford Rd, Shirley, Shirley 3846
Perry Greaves Ltd
Poplar Rd, 5716
Mrs D R L Howell (by appt only)
Squirrels, 579 Warwick Rd, 705 0990
A T Silvester & Sons Ltd
Warwick House, Warwick Rd, 0125
0888

SOMERTON (Som)
E S Pattemore & Sons
Market Sq, 422

SOULSBURY (Bucks)
Sid Jones
Lovett House, 349

SOUTHAMPTON (Hants)
Cottage Antiques
52 Northam Rd, 21546

J C Hingston
13 Northam Rd
Christine Leslie
8a Commercial Rd, 24931
L Moody
70 Bedford Pl, 22720
Northam Antiques
45-47 Northam Rd, 24993

SOUTHPORT (Lancs)
Blenkiron
45 Burton Arc, Lord St, 2637
Decor Galleries
92b Lord St
F D Glover
92b Lord St and 1 Market St, 56119
Jays Fine Art Dealers
4 Cambridge Arc, 55349
May Fayre Galleries
23 Wesley St, 4464
L J Metcalfe
5 Lord St, 2408
Marlow Antiques Ltd
41 Weld Rd, 66034
M E & A J Potts
Georgian Antique Shop, 49 Tulketh St,
3358 (trade only)
Westview Antiques
21 Aughton Rd, Birkdale, 66291
(by appt)

SOUTHSEA (Hants)
A R Challis Ltd
95 Palmerston Rd, Portsmouth 23838
Dolphin Antiques
15a Marmion Rd, Portsmouth 25165
G Downing
125 Albert Rd, Portsmouth 31070
George Edwardes
1 Festing Rd, Portsmouth 31794
A Fleming (Southsea) Ltd
The Clock Tower, Castle Rd,
Portsmouth 22934
Charles Hill
13 Marmion Rd
Jayell Antiques
172 Albert Rd, Portsmouth 31154
Kelmans
46 Marmion Rd, Portsmouth 32041
(trade only, Sat or by appt)
H L Leigh
48-50 Marmion Rd, Portsmouth 31744
Marmion Antiques
24 Marmion Rd, Portsmouth 24554
New & Old Antiques
198 Highlands Rd, Portsmouth 33563
Osborne Antiques
23 Osborne Rd, Portsmouth 25101
Radford Antiques
5 Marmion Rd, Portsmouth 22145
J Riley Antiques
54 Eastney Rd, Portsmouth 33444
Shop 16
16 Marmion Rd

George Ventham
146 Prince Albert Rd, Portsmouth
32030
Edmund Wheeler
69 Clarendon Rd, Portsmouth 31720

SOUTH CROYDON (Surrey)
Paul Keen
195 Brighton Rd, 1316

SOUTH WALSHAM (Norfolk)
Leo Pratt
The Old Curiosity Shop, South
Walsham 204

SOUTHWELL (Notts)
Cameron Antiques
The Chestnuts, Fiskerton,
Bleasby 236
Minster Antiques
17 Market Pl, 3137

SOUTHWOLD (Suffolk)
Mrs Field Antiques
Trinity St
L Finch
61 High St, 3271
David Lee
64 High St, 2576
Mella Antiques
Queen St
Took Antiques
Trinity St

SOWERBY BRIDGE (Yorks)
Art Boutique
45 Bolton Brow, Halifax 81186

SPALDING (Lincs)
N V Baker
22 Commercial Rd

SPROWSTON (Norfolk)
The Barn
12 School Lane, Norwich 48333

STAFFORD
Curiosity Corner
11 Wolverhampton Rd, 3674

STALLYBRIDGE (Dorset)
Ye Olde Curiosity Shoppe
531

STAMFORD (Lincs)
Ralph Cox
5 St Mary's Hill, 4159
W Dickerson (Antiques)
19 Scotgate, Oakham 2474
Ida Edinborough
4 St Mary's St, 3123

T S Hyde
59 Scotgate
Scotney & Son
13 St Mary.s Hill, 3151

STANSTED MOUNTFITCHET (Essex)
Linden House Antiques
3 Silver St, 2372
Sidney J Riches Antiques
Silver St, 3371
M R Simpson
Lower St, 3388

STEVENAGE (Herts)
Jeffries Antiques
The Ivy House, 36 High St,
52239

STEYNING (Sussex)
Hugh Williams Ltd
29 High St, 3268

STEWKLEY (Bucks)
Antiques & Things
60 High St North

STILLINGTON (Yorks)
M Plester
Main St, 203

STIRLING (Scotland)
Barron of Stirling Ltd
18 Baker St, 3693

STOCKBRIDGE (Hants)
A G O Hutchinson
The White House, 629
Philip & Ann Merridale
Bridge House, 51
Elizabeth Viney
Jacob's House, High St, 761
(by appt)

STOGUMBER (Som)
Derby House
207

STOKE-BY-NAYLAND (Suffolk)
The Mead House Antiques
Nayland 375
Prynne Hutton
Church St, Nayland 268

STOKE-ON-TRENT (Staffs)
Tunnicliffe's Antiques

STONE (Staffs)
The Upstairs Showrooms
2-3 Granville Chambers, Radford St,
700

STONY STRATFORD (Beds)
Dudley Hornsey
The Swan Antiques, 94 High St, 3090

STORRINGTON (Sussex)
The Old House Antiques
3187

STOURBRIDGE (Worcs)
Oldswingford Antiques
106 Hagley Rd, 5577
Simpson's of Stourbridge
Meriden House, 75 Market St, 5384

STOW-ON-THE-WOLD (Glos)
Christopher Clarke
The Square, 476
Cotswold Antiques Ltd
The Square
The Cotswold Galleries
The Square, 586
Fosse Way Antiques
Sheep St, 658
Manor House Antiques
The Square, 379
Peter Nelson
The Square, 771
Anthony Sampson Antiques
Park St, 159
Stow Antiques
The Square, 377
Swell Antiques
Lower Swell, 789

STRATFORD ST MARY (Essex)
Riverside Chimes
Dedham 2184

STRATFORD-UPON-AVON (Warks)
Harris Antiques
43a Wood St, 2394
P J Horsfield
21 Henley St, 5400
Little Gallery
37 Henley St, 3742
Poet's Arbour
Sheep St, 3453
The Ruskin Gallery
11 Chapel St, 2940
John Wigington
31 Henley St, 2143 (trade only)

STRATTON (Glos)
Syrena House
1 Cheltenham Rd, Cirencester 2755

STREATLEY-ON-THAMES (Berks)
E Fulford
Vine Cottage, High St,
Goring-on-Thames 391

STREET (Som)
The Ditty Box
196a High St
L Dicks
10a High St, 3680

STRETTON (Rutland)
The Old Greetham Inn
Great North Rd, Castle Bytham 340

STROUD (Glos)
A W England & Sons
Lower St, 3262
Gnome Cottage
55-57 Middle St, 3669

STUDLEY (Warks)
Prospect Antiques
Chester House, 2494
Royal Antiques
33 Redditch Rd, 2250

STURMINSTER NEWTON (Dorset)
Marshall Shrubb Antiques
3 Market Cross, 215

SUDBURY (Suffolk)
Ancient & Modern East Anglia Ltd
1-3 Friars St, 3185
Joan Coster
32-34 Friar St, 3075
Golden Age Antiques
Bridge House, Ballingdon, 2279
W C Nunn
3-4 Church St, 2352

SUTTON (Surrey)
Vera Bird
50 Sherwood Park Rd, 642 8188 (by appt)

SUTTON COLDFIELD (Warks)
H & R L Parry Ltd
23 Maney Corner, Birmingham Rd, 1178
Thoman Coulborn & Sons
Vesey Manor, 3974

SWAFFHAM (Norfolk)
The Antique Shop
66-68 London St, 697
H Blain
50 London St, 431
Mary Hayes
9 London St, Watton 754
Reiss Howard
Orwell House, Station Rd, 449
Mangate Antiques
9 Mangate St, 655
Manor Farm Antiques
on A47, 395
R W & J M White
Wentworth House, London St, 677

SWANAGE (Dorset)
Bishops of Swanage
31 Station Rd, 3245
Manwell Galleries
Seafront, 3001
Michael & Susan Yates Antiques
The Old Forge, 273a High St, 3319

SWANSEA (Glam)
Roger Hughes
13 Dilwyn St, 56673
P H James Antiques
74a-75 High St, 50126

SWINTON (Lancs)
The Armourers Shop
20 Chovey Rd
A & L Perry
592 Bolton Rd, Pendlebury and
37 Moorside Rd, 3735

TAKELEY (Essex)
Elkin Mathews Ltd
Taylors, 312
Treasure Trove
412

TATTERSHALL (Lincs)
J H & W G Millhouse
Market Pl, Coningsby 225

TAUNTON (Som)
C W Atkins & Co
90-92 Wellington Rd, 2660
The Gallery
Old Rectory House, Halse, Bishops
Lydeard 415
Gibbs & Manning
7 and 9 Billet St, 2577
Grange Court Antiques
Corfe, Blagdon Hill 498
Jean Jones Antiques
18 Paul St, 81996
F J Langford
15 East Reach, 817198
Staplegrove Lodge Antiques
Staplegrove, 81153
Treasure Chest Ltd
21 Staplegrove Rd, 3095

TAVISTOCK (Devon)
Number Three Antiques
Drake Rd, off Bedford Sq, 3576 and
2616
Vanity Fare
Abbey Arch, Court Gate, Bedford Sq,
2773

TEIGNMOUTH (Devon)
Teignmouth Antiques
10 Fore St

TENBURY WELLS (Worcs)
Temeside Antiques
55-57 Teme St, 633
Antiques
Worcester Rd, Burford

TENBY (Pembroke)
Audrey Bull
15 Upper Frog St, Saundersfoot 3425
Starboard Light Antiques
Cob Lane, Tudor Sq, 2098

TENTERDEN (Kent)
Antique Galleries
1a High St, 2060
Rika Hellard
The Quaint Conceit, 122 High St, 112
Nicholls Antiques
118 High St, 2455
Spinning Wheel

TETBURY (Glos)
Chatelaine Antiques
35 Long St, 748
Joane Crarer Antiques
Nelson House, 36 Long St, 660
J & B Ashley Kimber
20 Long St
Meyrick Neilson of Tetbury
Avon House, Market Pl, 201
John Nicholson
1 London Rd, 271
The Tetbury Furniture Co Ltd
6 Long St, 474
Two Toad's Antiques
28 Long St, 222

TEWKESBURY (Glos)
Abbey Antiques
62 Church St, 2378
Gainsborough House Antiques
Church St, 3072

THAME (Oxon)
George Newitt
11-12 High St, 125

THAMES DITTON (Surrey)
The White Shop
Portsmouth Rd, 398 4533/0330

THATCHAM (Berks)
The Crown House
High St, 3335

THAXTED (Essex)
The Recorder's House Antiques
438
Thaxted Galleries
1 Newbiggin St, 350
Turpins Antiques
Dick Turpin's Cott, 495

145

THURSO (Scotland)
The Ship's Wheel
2 Traill St, 2485

TIDDINGTON (Warks)
Heirlooms
30 Marn Rd, Stratford 4503

TIDESWELL (Derby)
Aladdin's Cave
Queen St, 479

TINGEWICK (Beds)
Tingewick Antiques
The Antique Shop, Main St

TITCHFIELD (Hants)
Harp Antiques
36–38 South St, 2533
B J & P B Manley
6–8 South St
Titchfield Antiques
10 High St, 3348

TIVERTON (Devon)
Holme Place Ltd
Holme Pl, Oakford, Oakford 332

TONBRIDGE (Kent)
Lawson Antiques Ltd
165 High St, 2183

TONG (Shrops)
Doveridge House Antiques
Neach Hill, Long Lane, Albrighton 3131

TOPSHAM (Devon)
Elizabeth Allnutt Antiques
13 Fore St, 4224

TORQUAY (Devon)
Abbey Rd Antiques
45 Abbey Rd, 21744
C & D O'Donoghue
Erith Mount, Higher Erith Rd, 23567
M H & J M Nott
Glenfield, Old Torwood Rd, 23039
Russell's (Antiques) Ltd
14 Fleet St, 22781
Silver Pixie
70–79 Fore St, St Mary Church, 39662

*A period street at the Stately
Antique Market, Woburn Abbey*

Miss I D Skinner
17 and 21 Torwood St, 27119
Stockman Antiques
250 Union St, Torre, 25778

TORRINGTON (Devon)
Castle Antiques
South St, 2232

TOTLAND BAY (Isle of Wight)
Antiques & Curios
2 Granville Ct, The Broadway, Totland,
Freshwater 2795

TOTNES (Devon)
Antiques & Decor (Herbert Bavington)
Top O'Town, 18 Cistern St

TOWCESTER (Northants)
Sarah's Cottage Antiques
147 Watling St West, 550
Ron Green of Towcester
Watling St, 467
Barbara Spry Antiques
161 Watling St, 639

TOWYN (Merioneth)
Market Hall Antiques
369

TREDINGTON (Warks)
Shirley Brown
The Green, Shipston-on-Stour 570

TRING (Herts)
John Bly
50 High St, 3030
Chapel House
Frogmore St, 3004

TRURO (Cornwall)
The Antique Shop
13 Pydar St, 2876

146

Alan Bennett
15–16 St Marys St, 3296
Miscellanea (Cornwall) Ltd
15 River St, 3793

TUNBRIDGE WELLS (Kent)

Chapel Antiques
Chapel Place
The Chair Shop
6 London Rd, 27364
The Coach & Horses
31a The Pantiles
S T & A A Duggan
38 Mount Ephraim, 22735
Gore-Langton
5 Castle St, 26373
David Kent
13 Langton Rd, 20372
Leonard Lassalle
21 The Pantiles, 31645
Littleton (Antiques) Ltd
35 Crescent Rd, 26002
Ye Olde Chequers
39 Crescent Rd, 27536
Meraud Mason
5 Neville St, 26776
The Pantiles Antiques Ltd
23 The Pantiles, 27926
Merlin Pennink
27 The Pantiles, 25825
Ann Spear
4 Nevill St, 26089
Leonard Strawson
39–41 The Pantiles, 30607

TWICKENHAM (Middx)

Marble Hill Antiques
229b Richmond Rd
Phelps Ltd
129–135 St Margarets Rd, 892 1778

TWYFORD (Berks)

Braemar
Wargrave Rd, Carlisle Corner, 115

TWYFORD (Hants)

Gladys Cain
High St, 3484

UBBESTON (Suffolk)

Chessman Antiques
The Old Rectory, 342

UCKFIELD (Sussex)

Red Tiles Antiques
High St, 118

UPPINGHAM (Rutland)

C H Thorpe
High St, 2116

UXBRIDGE (Middx)

H R S Turner
2 Cross St, 33035
University Prints
The Cedars, 65 High St, 35971

WAINFLEET (Lincs)

The Antique Centre
1 Spilsby Rd, 489

WAKEFIELD (Yorks)

P A M Cooper
11–13 Warrengate, 3317

WALLINGFORD (Berks)

Antiques (Ronald Windle)
Crowmarsh Gifford, 2518
Eagle House
16 High St, 2429
Anthony J Lester
Old Brewery House, High St, 3552

147

Henry J Madgwick
Old Brewery House, High St, 3486
Pennyfarthing
Crowmarsh Gifford, 3470
Summers, Davis & Son Ltd
Calleva House, 2284

WALLINGTON (Surrey)
Mrs Norman Knott
1 Holmwood Gdns, 8274 (by appt)

WALSALL (Staffs)
Keith Mallin Antiques
79 Ablewell St, Arboretum 437
Roberts Antiques
91 Ablewell St, 24306

WALSINGHAM (Norfolk)
Antiques
High St

Domingo's
High St, 381
C F U Fisher
17 High St, 223

WALTHAM CROSS (Herts)
J de Haan & Son Ltd
Harold House, 73 High St, 22756
(trade only)

WALTON-ON-THE-HILL (Surrey)
Country Shop
20 Walton St, Tadworth 3393
A Henning
48 Walton St, Tadworth 3337
Regency House (Walton) Antiques Ltd
Walton St, Tadworth 3060
Leslie Stedman
49 Walton St, Tadworth 2507

Patricia Mahony

WALTON-ON-THE-NAZE (Essex)

Pier Antiques
26 The Parade

WAREHAM (Dorset)

Eve's Casket
32 South St, 2810

WARMINSTER (Wilts)

Peter Bulkley
Green Farm, Crockerton

WARRINGTON (Lancs)

One Black Jane
Newton Lane, Preston Brook, Norton Brook 443

WARWICK (Warks)

H H Bray
9 Jury St, 42791
Robinsons (Quinneys of Warwick) Ltd
9 Church St and 7 High St, 42843
A T Silvester & Sons Ltd
2–4 High St, 42972

WASHINGTON (Sussex)

Chanctonbury Gallery
Clematis Cottage, Ashington 233

WATERINGBURY (Kent)

Antiques
Japonica Cottage, Tonbridge Rd, 340

WATLINGTON (Oxon)

Philadelphia Lee
Old Bank House, 223
Thimbles Antiques
238

WATTON (Norfolk)

Clarence House Antiques
High St, 767

WEDNESBURY (Staffs)

J Glaze
25–26 High Bullen, 0196

WEEDON (Northants)

Janos Aladics
66 High St, 574
Peter Proudfoot
38–40 High St, 482
Proudfoot & McNiven
62 High St, 472
A B Urquhart
62 High St, 207

WELLESBOURNE (Warks)

John Taylor
29 Warwick Rd, 579

Mrs Jennings
Warwick Rd
I E Neely
3 Bridge St

WELLINGTON (Som)

Georgian House Antiques
17 High St, 2171
Oxenhams
82a Mantle St, 2592

WELLS (Som)

Yvonne Hamilton
8 Sadler St, 2528
Mitre Antiques
17 Sadler St, 2607
Edward Nowell
21–23 Market Pl, 2415

WELSHPOOL (Montgomery)

R E Anderson & Son
5–6 High St, 3340

WELWYN (Herts)

Mac & Me (Antiques) Ltd
24 High St, 4710
The Old Chequers Antiques
Church St,
5451
Leslie Wenn
Prospect Pl, 4089

WEM (Shrops)

Grocott Picture Gallery
Noble St, 2584

WENDENS AMBO (Essex)

The Old Forge
Newport 233

WENDOVER DEAN (Bucks)

Bowood Antiques
Wendoverdean Farm, Wendover 2113

WEST BURTON (Yorks)

Long Farthing Antiques
West Burton, nr Leyburn, Aysgarth 213

WEST LISS (Hants)

C H Dunkley
The Malt House, Farnham Rd, 3104
Greentrees Antiques
3328

WESTBURY (Wilts)

Brian Craik Ltd
The Old Vicarage, Dilton Marsh, Westbury 2265

WESTERHAM (Kent)

L Davison Antiques
The Green, 3297

W & E Fuller
2a High St
John C Hook
3 The Green, 2161
Constance Johns
99 High St, 3257
Lillian Letts (Antiques) Ltd
High St, 2182
D H Sargeant
21 The Green, 2130
Walker's of Westerham
21 High St, 3055

WESTWELL (Kent)
The Mill House
Charing 500 (pref by appt)

WEYBRIDGE (Surrey)
Church House Antiques
42 Church St, 42190
R Saunders
71 Queens Rd, 42601
Stubbs
28 Daneswood Cl, 47136

WEYMOUTH (Dorset)
The Curiosity Shop
St Alban House, 6832
Quarries
22 St Edmund St, 3267

WHALLEY (Lancs)
Abbey Antique Shop
45 King St, 3139
Barrow Antiques
Barrow, 3511

WHATLINGTON (Sussex)
Chapel Antiques
Sedlescombe 272

WHEATHAMPSTEAD (Herts)
Collins Antiques
Corner House, 3111

WHITBY (Yorks)
Eskdale Antiques
96 Church St

WHITCHURCH (Bucks)
Deerstalker Antiques
Whitchurch 505

WHITCHURCH (Herefords)
Kathleen Macready Antiques
The Forge

WHITCHURCH (Shrops)
Church St Antiques
Church St, Great Bolas 213
The Old Curiosity Shop
17 Watergate St

J R Curtis
6 Doddington
F W Hancock
Moss Side, 4 Brownlow St, 2567

WHITE COLNE (Essex)
Compton-Dando
Berewyk Hall, Earls Colne 200

WHITEHAVEN (Cumberland)
Owen Kelly
9–11 New St and 72 Duke St, 2879

WICKHAM (Hants)
E F Scott
Old Timbers, The Square, 3044

WICKHAM MARKET (Suffolk)
The Old Crown
Framlingham 328

WICKWAR (Glos)
Bell Passage Antiques
38 High St
Chestnut Cottage Antiques
72 Sodbury Rd, 338
Victorian House Antiques
Station Rd, 205

WIDLEY (Hants)
B Young
10 Dell Cl, Cosham 71452

WIGAN (Lancs)
E Sheargold
130–130a Standishgate, 42980

WILLERBY (Yorks)
Antiques & Arts
28 Main St, 653688

WILMSLOW (Cheshire)
Peter Bosson Antiques
4 Church St, 27857
N H Trace
31 Manchester Rd, 25182

WILTON (Wilts)
Norman Newport
The Old Thatched House, 37–39 West St, 3340

WIMBLEDON (Surrey)
Anne Delaney
96 High St, Wimbledon Common, SW19, 946 7649

WIMBORNE MINSTER (Dorset)
The Brass Skillet
West St

Zona Dawson
The Antique Shop, 17 The Cornmarket, 3983
Metcalfe Jackson
Trumpeters, West St, 3327
The Quarter Jack Antiques Ltd
6 Cook Row, 3092

WINCANTON (Som)
Gabriel Olive
7 Church St, 3373
B Sainsbury
17 High St, 2289

WINCHCOMBE (Glos)
Elizabeth Mary Antiques
74–76 Gloucester St, 741
J Holmes & Co
Jacobean House, 282
Mrs Muriel Lindsay
Queen Anne House, 319

WINCHESTER (Hants)
R & K Behrens
15–17 Bridge St, 61807
G H Bell
32a The Square, 4505
Bernfeld Bros Ltd
God Begot House, 101 High St, 4589
J W Blanchard Ltd
12 Jewry St, 4547/2041
Brooks of Winchester
3 St Thomas St, 4545
Collectors Corner
1–2 The Square, 4686
Philip King
23 Southgate St, 3662
Look
41 Middlebrook St, 63731
Olive Parry
24a Jewry St, 3829
Ivy Spicer
Redruth, 96 St Cross, 3470
H J L Viney & Daughter Ltd
23–27 Chesil St, 4748
Mrs K M Shaw
28a The Square
Mrs Sheppard
11 The Square, 2911
R A Ettrick Welford
22 The Square, 3881

WINDERMERE (Westmorland)
Mrs Robinson
2 St Michaels Villas

WINDSOR (Berks)
Guy Bousfield
57/58 Thames St, 64575
Cherub Antiques
8 Church St, 60157
Cyril Hoy
17–19 Kings Rd, 65555 (Thurs to Sat only)

Nell Gwynn's House
5 Church St, 66246
Richard J Piner Ltd
Market Cross House, 51 High St, 60616
H H Roberts
Castle Studio, 66268

WINEHAM (Sussex)
Ena Friend-James
Grovelands, Bolney 311

WINGHAM (Kent)
Forge House Antiques
Bridge House Antiques
Antiques
88 High St, 355

WINSLOW (Bucks)
R Parker
High St

WINTERBOURNE DAUNTSEY (Wilts)
Winterbourne Antiques
The Manor House, Winterbourne Gunner 334

WISBECH (Cambs)
Joan Ing Antiques
55 Elm Rd, 3129

WITHINGTON (Glos)
Withington Antiques
287

WITNEY (Oxon)
Robert Mills
99 High St

WIVENHOE (Essex)
The Antique Galleries
523

WIVLESCOMBE (Devon)
Norman Follett
9 West St

WOBURN (Bucks)
Woburn Antique Galleries
19 Market Pl, 200
Christopher Sykes
11 Market Pl, 259

WOKINGHAM (Berks)
The Pandora Box
Shute End, 723
Alfred C White & Son
24 Broad St, 1042

WOLSELEY BRIDGE (Staffs)
Wolseley Bridge Antiques
Little Haywood 296

151

WOLVERHAMPTON (Staffs)

Chapel Ash Galleries
68 Chapel Ash, 25257
Wesley Henn Antiques Ltd
46–48 Chapel Ash, 22404
Ye Olde Curiosity Shoppe
St Peter's Chambers, Lich-Gate, Queen Sq, 23519

WOODBRIDGE (Suffolk)

Anvil Antiques
Station Rd, Melton, 2960
Simon Carter Gallery
23 Market Hill, 2242
Joan Chennell
The Old Forge, The Street, Melton, 3383
Anthony Hurst
13 Church St, 2500
Betty Meysey-Thompson
10 Church St, 2144

WOODHALL SPA (Lincs)

James Best (Furnishers) Ltd
The Broadway, 3113

WOODHOUSE EAVES (Leics)

Richard H Everard
Mapledene, 291 (by appt)
Esme Godkin
Burleigh, 4 Nanhill Dr, 538

WOODSTOCK (Oxon)

Peter Bye
16 Oxford St, 253
John Wells
24 Oxford St, 239
Wheeler of Woodstock
22 Oxford St, 206
Woodstock Galleries
9 Park St, 7305

WOOLHAMPTON (Berks)

The Old Bakery
2116
The Old Corner Shop
3256

WORCESTER (Worcs)

Antique Market
57 Sidbury
Doherty Bullock Bygones Worcester
Danesbury House, 55 Sidbury, 23132
Cavalier Antiques Ltd
King Charles House, New St, 27284
A V Harrison
61 Sidbury, 25671
M Lees & Son
Tower House, Severn St, 26620
A J Philpott
34 Sidbury, 24804

George Simons
61 The Tything
Mr & Mrs Stirling-Brown
12 The Tything
A Taylor
32 Sidbury
T Tolley
26 College St, 26632
Wyatt of Worcester
The Barn, Hawford, Fernhill Heath 221

WORTHING (Sussex)

A Biscoe
120–122 Montague St, 2489
Godden of Worthing Ltd
15–19 Crescent Rd, 5958 (trade only)
Christopher Phillips
76 Heene Rd, 30877
The White House (Worthing) Ltd
87 Rowlands Rd, 30844
H Williams Ltd
126 Montague St, 918

WOTTON-UNDER-EDGE (Glos)

(near Nailsworth)
Bell Passage Antiques
38 High St, Wickwar 251
Cotswold House Antiques
16 Bradley St, 3159

WREXHAM (Denbigh)

Peter Bailey
280 Chester Rd, 2648
(trade only)
Percy Goddard
35 Kings Mills Rd, 2368

WRINGTON (Som)

Wrington Antiques
Tanners, 200

WROXHAM (Norfolk)

T C S Brooke
The Grange, 2644

YARMOUTH (Isle of Wight)

Solent Antiques
The Square, 253

YEOVIL (Som)

L Dicks
115 Middle St, 5811
Phyllis Gossage Ltd
6 Westminster St, 3964
Edgar Vincent & Son
The Casket, 103 Middle St, 58

YORK

Antiques
5 and 45 The Shambles, 54821
D & D Butler
60 Low Petergate, 53278

Barbara Cattle
45 Stonegate, 23862
Coulter Galleries
34 The Horseshoe, Dringhouses, 66820
The Gazebo
Kings Sq, 68398
W F Greenwood & Sons Ltd
37 Stonegate, 23864
Henry Hardcastle Ltd
51 Stonegate, 23401
Ron Hope
Silverdale, 566 Huntington Rd, 68567
Robert Morrisson
Adams House, Petergate, 23333
M Plester Antiques
57 Low Petergate, 53428
Priory Antiques
12 Priory St, 23264

Stapylton House
137 Fulford Rd, 58488 (Tues, Fri, Sat)
Treasure Seekers
28 Walmgate, 54058

YOXALL (Staffs)
J C E & N I Armson
The Hollies, 352
The Antique Shop
266

YOXFORD (Suffolk)
Phoebe Cobbold
Coach House Cott, 302
Golden Age Antiques
Budge House, Ballingdon, 2279
W C Nunn
3-4 Church St, 2352

London dealers

For reasons of space, I am unable to list each and every London dealer in antiques. They number more than a thousand, and we felt that a simple list would not be of much assistance to our readers. We have, however, listed all those dealers mentioned in specialist chapters. The names and addresses of London picture galleries recommended can be found immediately following the glossary of London antique dealers.

Norman Adams Ltd
8-10 Hans Rd, SW3, 589 5266
Albert Amor Ltd
37 Bury St, St James's SW1, 930 2444
Anglo-Persian Carpet Co (London) Ltd
6 South Kensington Station Arcade, SW7, 589 5457
Antique City
45 Crawford Pl, NW1, 723 2621
Antique Hypermarket Ltd
26-40 Kensington High St, W8, 937 6911

The Antique Porcelain Co Ltd
149 New Bond St, W1, 629 1254/5
The Antique Supermarket
4 Barrett St, W1, 486 1439
Antiques Corner Ltd (N Stelman)
104 Mount St, W1, 499 5558 and (priv) 727 4345
M & J Appleby
57 George St, W1, 486 0930
A Arditti
12b Berkeley St, W1, 629 0885
Asprey and Co Ltd
165-9 New Bond St, W1, 493 6767

G Austin & Sons Ltd
19 Peckham Rye and 39–41 Brayards
Rd, SE15, 639 3163

Au Vieux Paris
28 Knightsbridge, SW1, 235 4192

Ayer & Co (Antiques) Ltd
130 Mount St, W1, 493 2341

E A Baker
7 New Cavendish St, W1, 935 0184

A H Baldwin and Sons Ltd
1–11 John Adam St, WC2, 839 2455

Barling of Mount St Ltd
112 Mount St, W1, 499 2858

Baroque Corner
139 Portobello Rd, W11, 286 9985

Bayley's Galleries
8 Princes Arcade, Piccadilly, SW1,
734 0180

Bayswater Antiques Market
122 Bayswater Rd, W2, 229 0051

J and A Beare Ltd
179 Wardour St, W1, 437 1449

Beauchamp Antiques Ltd
39 Beauchamp Pl, SW3, 589 1335

Beauchamp Galleries
8 Beauchamp Pl, SW3, 589 5716

Peter Bernard Ltd
39 Elystan St, SW3, 584 1105

Benardout and Benardout
7 Thurloe Pl, SW7, 584 7658

Big Deal
62 Princedale Rd, W11

David Black
96 Portland Rd, W11, 727 2566

H Blairman and Sons Ltd
36 New Bond St, W1, 493 0444

N Bloom and Son Ltd
39–40 Albemarle St, Piccadilly, W1,
629 5060

Bluett and Sons
48 Davies St, W1, 629 4018

The Bond Street Antique Centre
124 New Bond St, W1

Bond Street Silver Galleries
111–112 New Bond St, W1

Joanna Booth
247 Kings Rd, SW3, 352 8998

Peter Boswell (Arts) Ltd
67–69 Beak St, W1, 734 7909

D Bouldstridge Ltd
47 Lower Belgrave St, SW1, 730 7548

J H Bourdon-Smith Ltd
25a Conduit St, W1, 629 0434

Richard Bowman Ltd
355 Oxford St, W1, 629 5203

Aubrey Brocklehurst
124 Cromwell Rd, South Kensington,
SW7, 373 0319

W G T Burne (Antique Glass) Ltd
11 Elystan St, SW3, 589 6074

Cale Antiques
24 Cale St, SW3, 589 6146 and (priv)
286 0928

Cameo Corner Ltd
26 Museum St, WC1, 636 0401

Camerer Cuss and Co
54–56 New Oxford St, WC1, 636 8968

J & K Cameron Antiques
507 Upper Richmond Rd, SW14,
770 5721

Jack Casimir Ltd
The Brass Shop, 23 Pembridge Rd, W11,
727 8643

Chelsea Antique Market
253 King's Rd, SW3, 352 9695

Chelsea Antiques
336 King's Rd, SW3, 352 3847

Chester Antiques Ltd
239 King's Rd, SW3, 352 1415

China Choice
163b Kentish Town Rd (Kelly St), NW1
485 7793

Church Street Galleries Ltd
77 and 64a Kensington Church St, W8,
937 2461

Ciacimino
309 King's Rd, SW3, 352 3941

Clewes & Makin
588 King's Rd, SW6, 736 3955

Collet's Chinese Gallery
40 Gt Russell St, WC1, 580 7538

Collingwood (Jewellers) Ltd
48 Conduit St, W1, 734 2656

A Cook
13–16 St Christopher's Pl, Wigmore St,
W1, 935 7244

Corbitt & Hunter
175 Piccadilly, London, W1

Corner Cupboard
14 Pierrepont Arcade, N1, 226 4539

Cortell & Company Ltd
11 Charterhouse St, EC1, 242 3987

Coxson Antiques Ltd
63 Cadogan Pl, SW1, 235 1014

J Crotty and Son Ltd
157 Greyhound Rd, W6, 385 1789

T Crowther and Son Ltd
282 North End Rd, Fulham, SW6,
385 1375/7

The Curio Shop
Shepherd Market, W1

C J Dade
44 Pimlico Rd, SW1, 730 3001

Peter Dale Ltd
11 and 12 Royal Opera Arcade, Pall Mall,
SW1, 930 3695

A B Davis
89–91 Queensway, W2, 229 2777

Cecil Davis Ltd
3 Grosvenor St, New Bond St, W1,
499 3130

Walter Davis
St Martin's Lane, WC2

De Havilland (Antiques) Ltd
14 Grafton St, W1, 493 4392

Delieb Antiques Ltd
Ely House, 13 Charterhouse St, EC1,   ·
242 4947

Delomosne & Son Ltd
4 Campden Hill Rd, W8, 937 1804

Richard Dennis
144 Kensington Church St, W8, 727 2061

E Dent
Pall Mall, W1

Daniel Desbois and Sons
51 Carey St, WC2, 405 7935

Esta Dickson (Antiques) Ltd
123 Gloucester Rd, SW7, 373 2934

P G Dodd and Son Ltd
42 Cornhill, EC3, 626 8616

Dodo
185 Westbourne Grove, W11,
BAYswater 3132

Dolphin Antiques
2b Englands Lane, NW3, 722 7003

Dombey, Philip and Bernard
174 Kensington Church St, W8,
229 7100

Michel Dumez-Onof
90–92 Pimlico Rd, SW1, 730 6626

M Ekstein Ltd
90 Jermyn St, SW1, 930 2024

A S Embden
Flat 8, Hector Court, Cambalt Rd, SW15,
789 1609

E Fairclough (Arms) Ltd
25 Conduit St, W1, 493 3946

Falks Ltd
91 Farringdon Rd, EC1, 405 7654

Chris Farlowes Militaria Vault
Boutique Arcade, Camden Passage, N1,
359 0501

Fernandes & Marche
80 Islington High St, N1, 837 8768

Filkins and Co
175 Old Brompton Rd, SW5

Fisher Gallery Ltd
18a Duchess Mews, Mansfield St, W1,
636 9779

E L Fitzroy
97 Jermyn St, SW1, 839 4853

Folio Fine Art Ltd
6 Stratford Pl, W1, 493 9104

Miss Fowler
1a Duke St, Manchester Sq, W1,
935 5187

Peter Francis
37 Beauchamp Pl, Knightsbridge, SW3,
589 4243

S Franses
71–73 Knightsbridge, SW1, 235 1888/9

A Fredericks (Chelsea) Ltd
265–7 Fulham Rd, SW3, 352 2188

C Fredericks and Son
76 Old Brompton Rd, SW7, 589 5847

Charles Frodsham and Co Ltd
173 Brompton Rd, SW3, 589 1073

L Gallindos
110 Chepstow Rd, W2, 229 6177

Garner and Marney Ltd
41–43 Southgate Rd, N1, 226 1535

T E Gascoigne
79 Albany St, NW1, 387 3158

Gay Antiques
1 Beauchamp Pl, SW3, 584 9615

Gee Bee Antiques
Brompton Rd, SW1

P C L German
125 Edgware Rd, W2, 723 9342

Giannitni Antiques Ltd
97 Lower Sloane St, SW1, 730 8516

Giblin & Hirst
59 Pembridge Rd, W11, 727 9364

Gillingham Brooks
345 Fulham Rd, SW10, 352 2623

Glaisher and Nash Ltd
Lowndes Lodge, Cadogan Pl, SW1,
235 2285/6

Gloria Antica
170 Brompton Rd, SW3, 589 0367

D Goodchild & Son Ltd
Reliance House, 51 Great Eastern St,
EC2, 739 4161

Nicholas Gorevic
97 Jermyn St, SW1, 930 1589

A E Gould & Sons (Antiques) Ltd
193 King's Rd, SW3, 352 8739

Gregory and Co (Bruton Street) Ltd
27 Bruton St, W1, 629 2608/10
and 2066

Grejoron Antiques
7 Pierrepoint Row, Islington, N1,
226 8211

Guinevere Antiques Ltd
578 King's Rd, SW6, 736 2917

J Haim and Co
31 Brook St, W1, 629 6300

M Hakim
4 Royal Arcade, Old Bond St, W1,
629 2643

155

John Hall David MacWilliams
17 Harrington Rd, SW7, 584 1307

Victor Hall
735 Fulham Rd, SW6, 736 2128

Halliday's (Antiques) Ltd
28 Beauchamp Pl, SW3, 589 5534

Hamish (London) Ltd
335 Fulham Rd, SW10, 352 9431

H R Hancock and Sons
37 Bury St, St James's, SW1, 930 6670

Hancocks and Co (Jewellers) Ltd
9 Vigo St, W1, 734 1174

Gordon Hand and Co
18 Chepstow Mansions, Westbourne
Grove, W2, 229 0322

Keith Harding Antiques
93 Hornsey Rd, N7, 607 6181 (priv)
607 3761

James Hardy and Co
235 Brompton Rd, SW3, 589 5050

M Harris and Sons
44–52 New Oxford St, WC1,
636 2121/2/3

W R Harvey and Co Ltd
69 Chalk Farm Rd, NW1, 485 1504

J F Hayward
17 Piccadilly Arcade, SW1, 493 5082

A Henning
61 George St, Portman Sq, W1,
935 7858

Hesters Carpets
75 Duke St, SW1, 629 6415

Miss A D Hodson
6 Park Walk, SW10, 352 0627

Hoff Antiques Ltd
66a Kensington Church St, W8,
229 5516 (priv) 272 6542

E Hollander
80 Fulham Rd, SW3, 589 7239

Huggins and Horsey Ltd
26 Beauchamp Pl, SW3, 584 1685

M H Impey
172 Walton St, SW3, 584 3796

Jellinek & Vermoutier
131a Kensington Church St, W8,
727 8424

Jeremy Ltd
255 King's Rd, SW3, 352 3127/8

C John
70 South Audley St, W1, 493 5288

Junk City
36–40 Bell St, NW1

Alexander Juran & Co
74 New Bond St, W1, 629 2550 and
493 4484

H W Keil
27–29 Brook St, Bond St, W1, 629 6448

Kensington Market
49–53 Kensington High St, W8,
937 0296

Kenway Antiques
70 Kenway Rd, SW5, 373 1631

Kyrle Fletcher Antiques
85 Bourne St, Sloane Sq, SW1, 730 4944

The Lacquer Chest
75 Kensington Church St, W8,
937 1306

S Lampard and Son Ltd
32 Notting Hill Gate, W11, 229 5457
and (priv) 876 7526

Langfords Silver Galleries
11 Charterhouse St, EC1, 405 6401

T & S Lemkow
8/9 Pierrepont Arcade, N1, 226 2997

M P Levene Ltd
5 Thurloe Pl, SW7, 589 3755

Stanley Leslie
15 Beauchamp Pl, SW1, 536 2333

Stephen Lewis
192 Westbourne Grove, W11,
229 8748

Lloyds
16 Motcomb St, Belgrave Sq, SW1,
235 1010

London Silver Vaults
Chancery House, Chancery Lane, WC2,
242 3844

Lories Ltd
89b Wigmore St, W1, 935 7077

Ivar Mackay
4 Kensington Church Walk, W8,
937 0983 (priv) 3323

Mallet and Son (Antiques) Ltd
40 New Bond St, W1, 499 7411

Mallet at Bourdon House Ltd
2 Davies St, W1, 629 2444

D M and P Manheim
69 Upper Berkeley St, Portman Sq, W1,
723 6595

Mann and Fleming Ltd
120b Mount St, W1, 449 2770 and 2723

Marian Marks
171 Fulham Rd, SW3, 589 3353

Mayfair Village Antiques
19 Shepherd Market, W1, 493 4796

Mayflower Antiques
5 St Christopher's Pl, Wigmore St, W1,
935 9163

Mayorcas Ltd
38 Jermyn St, SW1, 629 4195

Mercury Antiques
1 and 1b Ladbroke Rd, W11, 727 5106

Sydney L Moss Ltd
51 Brook St, W1, 629 4670

Avice Mostyn Antiques Ltd
580 King's Rd, SW6, 736 7715

Dixon Mudd (Antiques) Ltd
4 New Cavendish St, W1, 935 2604

Richard Mundey
19 Chiltern St, W1, 935 5613

The Music Box Gallery
81 George St, W1, 935 4700

David B Newbon
56 Beauchamp Pl, SW3, 589 1369

Newman and Newman (Antiques)
Ltd
156 Brompton Rd, SW3, 589 5272 and
3793

Norman Newton (Military Antiques) Ltd
Tradition, 188 Piccadilly, SW1, 734 1352

D & H Oakley
53 Fulham High St, SW6, 736 4573

The Old Metalcraft Shop
194 Brompton Rd, SW3, 589 5001

The Old Pewter Shop
142 Brompton Rd, SW3, 589 7370

Marjorie Parr Galleries
285 King's Rd, SW3, 352 0768

Frank Partridge and Sons Ltd
144 New Bond St, W1, 629 0834/5

J Pearson-Smythe & Co
80 New King's Rd, SW6, 736 8699

Peel Antiques
131d Kensington Church St, W8, 727 8298

Peerage Antiques
29 Thayer St, W1, 486 9860

Perez (London) Ltd
112 Brompton Rd, SW3, 589 4411

Period Metals
25 and 27 Chalk Farm Rd, NW1, 485 1049

Persian Carpet Galleries
152 Brompton Rd, SW3, 584 5516

Howard Phillips
11a Henrietta Pl, W1, 580 9844

The Pine Chest
39 Pelham St, SW7, 589 1178

Pleasures of Past Times
11 Cecil Ct, Charing Cross Rd, WC2, 836 1142

Roger W Pliszka Antiques (UK) Ltd
77 Chepstow Rd, W2, 727 0833

Graham Pontet Ltd
102 Mount St, W1, 493 7552 also at
78 Jermyn St, SW1, 493 7552

H W Poulter
158 Fulham Rd, SW10, 373 4162

Pratt and Burgess Ltd
7 Old Brompton Rd, SW7, 589 8501

S R Preston
Campden St and 121b Kensington
Church St, W8, 727 4872

Prestons Ltd
91 Mount St, W1, 499 7644

Prides of London Ltd
179/180 Sloane St, SW1, 235 3080

A J Reffold and Partners Ltd
1 Pont St, SW1, 235 8351

The Room at the Back
22 Gt Windmill St, W1

Geoffrey Rose Ltd
77 Pimlico Rd, SW1, 730 3004

S L Antiques
371b Richmond Rd, Twickenham, 707 2986

St George's Galleries
39 George St, W1, 935 8478

Samads
47 Knightsbridge, SW1, 235 5712

B A Seaby Ltd
59–65 Great Portland St, W1, 580 3677

Lilli Segel
Hampstead Antique Emporium,
12 Heath Rd, NW3, 734 3297

Jean Sewell (Antiques) Ltd
3 and 4 Campden St, Kensington Church
St, W8, 727 3122

Shapland
207 High Holborn, WC1, 405 3507

S J Shrubsole Ltd
43 Museum St, WC1, 405 2712

David Slater
59 Chepstow Rd, W2 727 3336

John Sparks Ltd
128 Mount St, W1, 499 2265 and 1932

Spink and Son Ltd
5–7 King St, SW1, 930 5275

Spitz Antiques
561 King's Rd, SW6, 736 7574

Gerald Spyer and Son Ltd
237 Earls Court Rd, SW5, 370 2000

Charles Stewart (Antiques) Ltd
67 Wigmore St, W1, 935 3601 and 7081

Jacob Stodel
172 Brompton Rd, SW3, 589 1235

Philip Stone Ltd
12 Imperial Ct, Prince Albert Rd, NW8, 722 7303

Robin Symes
346a King's Rd, SW3, 352 2980

Them and Theirs
17a St Christopher Pl, W1, 935 0479

Things
72 Princedale Rd, W11

Through the looking glass
563 King's Rd, SW6, 736 7799

157

Tilley and Co (Antiques) Ltd
2 Symons St, Sloane Sq, SW3, 730 4753
Alan Tillman Antiques
6 Halkin Arcade, Motcomb St, SW1,
235 8235
Arthur G Tite
30 Burlington Arcade, W1, 629 3977 and
(priv 723 7592)
Tortoiseshell and Ivory House Ltd
24 Chiltern St, W1, 935 8031
Trad
Portobello Rd, W11
David Tremayne Ltd
320 King's Rd, SW3, 352 1194
D Tron
275 King's Rd, SW3, 352 5918
M Turpin
91 Old Brompton Rd, SW7, 584 6295
and 0449
Geoffrey Van & Co
15, 105 and 107 Portobello Rd, W11,
229 5577
A Vandekar
40 Staverton Rd, NW2, 459 3606
Joseph & Earle D Vandekar
138 Brompton Rd, SW3 589 8481
Victoriana
2 Church Rd, Wimbledon Village, SW19

The Vigo Art Galleries
6a Vigo St, Regent St, W1, 734 4951
Villafranca
140 Brompton Rd, SW3, 584 6499
Vita Juel
99 Kensington Church St, W8,
727 6751
William Walter (Antiques) Ltd
Silver Vaults, Chancery House, Chancery
Lane Safe Deposit, WC2, 242 3248/9
Wartski Ltd
138 Regent St, W1, 734 2794
Wernik Antiques Ltd
Dolphin Arcade, 157 Portobello Rd,
W11
Whytes
22 Park Rd, NW1, 723 3527
R Wilkinson & Son
11 High St, Wimbledon Common, SW19
946 0370
Temple Williams Ltd
3 Haunch of Venison Yard, Brook St, W1,
629 1486
Mary Wise
66a Honor Oak Rd, Forest Hill, SE23,
699 9634
Woodall & Emery
66 Great Portland St, W1, 636 3797

A Woodhouse and Son Ltd
The Silver Mouse Trap, 56 Carey St,
WC2, 405 2578
Greta Woolf
12 Pierrepoint Arcade, N1, 226 1880
Christopher's Wray's Lighting
Emporium
604 Kings Rd, SW6

Denys Wrey Ltd
45 Sloane St, SW1
Harriet Wynter
352 King's Rd, SW3, 352 6494
David Young
104 Chepstow Rd, W2, 229 0660
Lionel Young Antiques
93a Crawford St, W1, 723 4787

London picture dealers

Abbott and Holder
73 Castelnau, Barnes, SW13, 748 2416
Arthur Ackermann and Son Ltd
3 Old Bond St, W1, 493 3288
Thos Agnew and Sons Ltd
43 Old Bond St, W1, 629 6176/9 and
3 Albemarle St, WI
Albany Gallery
14 Masons Yard, Duke St, SW1,
839 6119
Arcade Gallery Ltd (Paul Wengraf)
28 Old Bond St, W1, 493 1879
Baynton-Williams
70 Old Brompton Rd, SW7, 584 7496/7
M Bernard
21 Ryder St, St James's, SW1, 930 6894
Herbert N Bier
2 Strathearn Pl, Hyde Park Sq, W2,
723 9522
Bernard Bivall
174a Kensington Church St, W8,
229 2988
Gallery Brod
24 St James's St
SW1, 839 3871/2
Bury Art Galleries
21 King St, St James's, SW1
Caelt Gallery
182 Westbourne Gr, W11, 279 9389
Ronald Cook Gallery
1st floor – Antique Hypermarket, W8,
937 2714
City Gallery (D Barclay)
2a Copthall Ct, Throgmorton St, EC2,
606 1568

J G Couper (Fine Arts) Ltd
9 Dering St, W1, 629 1578
Craddock and Barnard
32 Museum St, WC1, 636 3937
William R Drown
45 Dover St, W1, 493 4711
Duits Ltd
6 Duke St, St James's, SW1, 930 7440
Ferrers
9 Piccadilly Arcade, SW1, 493 6948
Fine Art Society Limited
148 New Bond St, W1, 629 5116
Folio Fine Art Ltd
6 Stratford Pl, W1, 493 9014
Fores Ltd
123 New Bond St, W1, 629 5319
Robert Frank
4 St James's St, SW1
930 2682
L Franklyn
3 The Croft, 62 Primrose Gdns, NW3,
722 6483
Frost and Reed Ltd
41 New Bond St, W1, 629 2457
Gallery Lasson
57 Jermyn St, SW1, 629 6981
Gooden and Fox Ltd
38 Bury St, St James's, SW1,
930 6422/3
Richard Green (Fine paintings) Ltd
36 Dover St, W1, 493 7997
Hallsborough Gallery
143 New Bond St, W1, 499 1923
Hazlitt Gallery (J M F Baer)
4 Ryder St, SW1, 930 6821

159

Heim Gallery (London) Ltd
59 Jermyn St, SW1, 493 0688

Holbein Galleries
70 Pimlico Rd, SW1, 730 8673

Henry Jacobs
1 Frognal Par, Finchley Rd, NW3,
435 1140/3311

W R H Jeudwine
28 Stafford Ter, W8, 937 1276

Oscar and Peter Johnson Ltd
Lowndes Lodge Gallery, Cadogan Pl,
SW1, 235 6464

Kaplan Gallery
6 Duke St, St James's, SW1, 930 8665

Arthur Kauffman
21 Grafton St, Bond St, W1, 493 4458

M Knoedler and Co Ltd
34 St James's St, SW1, 839 1641/2

Brian Koetser
38 Duke St, St James's, SW1, 930 6309

Leonard Koetser Ltd
13 Duke St, St James's, SW1, 930 9348

Paul Larsen
43 Duke St, St James's, SW1, 930 7597

Lefevre Gallery
30 Bruton St, W1, 629 2250

The Leger Galleries Ltd
13 Old Bond St, W1, 629 3538

Leggatt Bros
30 St James's St, SW1, 930 3772 and
3252

Leicester Galleries
4 Audley Square, South Audley St, W1,
629 1159

G M Lotinga Ltd
9a New Bond St, W1, 629 3952

MacConnel Mason and Son Ltd
19 Duke St, St James's, SW1, 930 3395

John McMaster
15–16 Royal Opera Arcade, Pall Mall,
SW1, 930 7679

Maltzahn Gallery Ltd
137 Fulham Rd, SW3, 584 8003

Manning Galleries Ltd
71 New Bond St, W1, 629 4629

Marlborough Fine Art Ltd
39 Old Bond St, W1, 629 5161

Mason Gallery
14 Masons Yard, St James, W1,
839 3875

John Mitchell and Son
8 New Bond St, W1, 493 7567

The Moorland Gallery
23 Cork St, Bond St, W1, 734 6961

M Newman Ltd
43a Duke St, St James's, SW1,
930 6068/9 and 1–3 Ryder St, SW1

Obelisk Gallery
15 Crawford St, W1, 486 9821

O'Hana Gallery
13 Carlos Pl, Grosvenor Sq, W1, 499 1562

**Old Masters Galleries (A M & E M
Wengraf)**
62 South Audley St, W1, 629 0223

Omell Galleries
22 Bury St, St James's, SW1, 839 4274

Hal O'Nians
6 Ryder St, St James's, SW1, 930 9392

The Parker Gallery
2 Albemarle St, Piccadilly, W1, 499 5906

Patterson and Shipman Ltd
19 Albemarle St, W1, 629 1910

Pawsey and Payne
1 Bury St, St James's, SW1, 930 4221

Rupert Preston Ltd
17 King St, St James's, SW1, 930 1794

Pulitzer Gallery
5 Kensington High St, W8, 937 2647

Quangle Prints
23 Beauchamp Pl, SW3, 589 7478

Arthur Reader
71 Charing Cross Rd, WC2, 437 2653

Roland Browse and Delbanco
19 Cork St, Old Bond St, W1, 734 7984

Rutland Gallery
266 Brompton Rd, SW3, 589 0139

Frank T Sabin
9 Albemarle St, W1, 499 5553

Schidlof Galleries
1 Holland Park Ct, Holland Park Gdns,
W14, 603 9480

Sifton, Praed & Co
The Map House, 67 St James St, SW1

The Sladmore Gallery
32 Bruton Pl, W1

Edward Speelman Ltd
175 Piccadilly, W1, 493 0657

Marshall Spink Ltd
18 Albemarle St, W1, 493 2575

John Stewart (Antiques) Ltd
41 Harrington Rd, SW7, 589 0683

Sutch and Martin
11 Bury Street, St James's, SW1,
930 2902

Temple Gallery
4 Yeomans Row, Brompton Rd, SW3,
589 3731

Arthur Tooth and Sons Ltd
31 Bruton St, W1, 499 6741

Tryon Gallery
41 Dover St, W1, 493 5161

Dennis Vanderkar Gallery
Duke St, St James's, SW1, 930 6994

William Ware Gallery
160 Fulham Rd, SW10, 370 5268

Wildenstein and Co Ltd
147 New Bond St, W1, 629 0602

LOWE *of* LOUGHBOROUGH

37-40 CHURCH GATE

Dealing in Antiques since 1885
Own car park
Telephone Loughborough 2554
Three miles from M1 (A512)
Open all week till
Friday 5.30 pm

162